PREFACE

When we first started planning this conference, we took two decisions which we knew would have significant consequences for this report. The first was to present a large number of submitted papers in parallel sessions, and the second was to have a variety of modes of presentation — papers, a symposium, workshops and an exhibition. In order to keep this report within reasonable bounds this meant that we could not print all the papers in full. Instead we asked each presenter of a paper and each member of the symposium to let us have a two-page abstract, and organisers of a workshop a one-page abstract. The symposium abstracts were circulated to all conference members in advance, so that the symposium itself could be devoted largely to discussion, and the abstracts of all the other papers were available at the conference so that members could read about those presentations which they were unable to attend, because of time clashes. We also provided photographs of speakers, so that members could identify them in the crowd.

The evaluation at the end of the conference made it clear that on the whole we pleased members, but that most people felt that the conference should have been longer in view of the wealth of material presented. That this extra time for papers should not be taken out of the time for informal meetings, which was substantial, was made abundantly clear.

The provision of workshops was an innovation that was clearly appreciated by those who attended them, but their clash with more formal sessions was not. The logistics of a conference time-table are not easy and we wonder whether members would have been more satisfied if we had drastically pruned the number of papers presented.

After the conference we invited one person from each session to let us have an extended version of his paper, and we asked one participant from each workshop to comment briefly on his experience; but apart from that this report prints the abstracts. For reasons of space we have also had to do some editorial work on the extended papers.

We appreciate that in doing all this we have undertaken a heavy responsibility, but we hope that the speed with which this report has appeared will exonerate us. We also hope that readers whose appetite has been whetted by the all too brief abstracts, will write to authors. We know that a number of them are publishing fuller versions of their work elsewhere.

Finally, we wish to thank the Association of University Teachers and the National Association of Teachers in Further and Higher Education for their generous support, which enabled the conference to run without a loss, and to the University of Surrey which allowed us to use a large number of its lecture rooms at no charge.

David Billing
Lewis Elton
Leo Evans
Kerren Simmonds
Joanna Tait

(Conference and Editorial Committee)

St[illegible] development in higher education

Papers presented at the twelfth annual conference of the Society in December 1976 at the University of Surrey

edited by Lewis Elton and Kerren Simmonds

Society for Research into Higher Education Ltd
at the University of Surrey, Guildford, Surrey, GU2 5XH
August 1977

Cover design by Direct Design (Bournemouth) Ltd

ISBN 0 900868 57 0

August 1977

CONTENTS

INTRODUCTION

by Professor L. R. B. Elton (University of Surrey, Institute for Educational Technology; Chairman, SRHE)

In the publicity before the conference, it was stated that 'The conference will concern itself with the professional training and development of academic and administrative staff in higher education. Among the questions to be considered are:

a) Should staff be trained?
b) If so, how?
c) Is there more to development than training?
d) How do the aims and responsibilities of an institution affect staff development?
e) What about retraining?

The intention is to concentrate on research and development and to use particular experiences for illustrative purposes'. How far did we succeed in our aim?

In the opening plenary session, there are three very different talks designed to exemplify the breadth of the subject that the conference proposed to tackle. Stoddart starts by giving an account of staff and course development as they apply in the main to polytechnics and colleges of education, although there is much there that is also relevant to universities. In a very different view, Hounsell, in looking at the processes of teaching and learning, suggests that we concentrate too much on teaching at the expense of learning. He outlines how research into learning may help, but makes it clear that much of this research lies in the future. Finally, Mirande provides an interesting analysis of the various structures of training courses and gives a glimpse of how another country approaches staff development.

Following the opening session, the conference broke into two very important parallel sessions. A symposium on staff development in the United Kingdom reveals interesting and significant differences between universities and polytechnics, while in a session devoted to practices abroad, Dressel explains the development of the American Doctor of Arts.

The rest of the programme broadly falls into two parts. Sessions 5 and 7 deal with techniques of staff development. Ramsden and Elton both show how staff can learn from an evaluation of their teaching, and Cox, in a most original contribution, illustrates that they can also learn from an evaluation of their learning in a staff development course. The three contributors to the small group session all in different ways advocate the use of small groups for the achievement of affective aims.

Sessions 4, 6 and 8 deal with matters of milieu and organization. Of particular note here are Rutherford's findings that many young staff resent and reject the suggestion of training, Rhodes's description of the conservative attitudes of students, and Startup's account which shows up the all-pervading influence of a Head of Department. In the final session, Cowan brings us full circle back to Mirande in analysing the form and content of training courses.

It has not been possible in this brief overview to mention every one of the speakers, and nothing has been said about the workshops and exhibition which proved so valuable. But let us ask our question again — how far did we achieve our aims? Matheson's evaluation makes it clear that members left the conference in a somewhat confused state, but this may well be at least to some extent because they were only able to sample a few of the offerings. Reading over the conference report as a whole one finds substantial answers to questions (a), (b), (c) and (d), although not to (e); there was much on academics and virtually nothing on administrators, there was a little on research, much on developments and illustrative experiences; blessedly little that was purely anecdotal. One is left with the impression that staff development in higher education is many faceted and that it is still looking for a sense of direction. Let us resolve to meet again in a few years time to see where we shall have got to.

1. OPENING PLENARY SESSION

Staff Development and Course Development in the Public Sector of Higher Education

J. Stoddart (Hull College of Higher Education)

Staff Development and Research on Teaching and Learning

D. Hounsell (University of Lancaster)

Principles Underlying University Teacher Courses

Dr. M.J.A. Mirande (University of Amsterdam)

STAFF DEVELOPMENT AND COURSE DEVELOPMENT IN THE PUBLIC SECTOR OF HIGHER EDUCATION

by J. Stoddart, Director, Hull College of Higher Education

My contribution is not given from the perspective of the researcher or of the teacher working within a teaching methods unit or staff development team, but is from that of an administrator responsible for the operation and development of a large college. It is based on experience of the public sector of higher education over the past twelve years and, in particular, educational institutions which have experienced a rapid change of role within a relatively short space of time. It is experience that has been shared by many in the Polytechnics and those colleges involved in advanced F.E. provision; it may have particular relevance for the many colleges of higher education now being established as a result of Government policy on teacher training.

I find it useful to distinguish between two types of college — those which, in the past ten years, have experienced growth in student numbers and yet have not been subject to radical change of purpose or structure, and those which have been subject to rapid and significant institutional change. In both types of college, it is commonly argued that staff development is principally a matter for the individual, that it is implicit in the assumption of academic tenure that an individual member of staff will keep pace with any necessary change by engaging in research and consultancy, attending conferences, seeking higher qualifications. The responsibility of the college is to provide a framework within which the individual can realise his potential and can engage in these types of activity. The role of college management is seen as ensuring that there is an adequate budget for conferences and courses, responding to requests for secondments and sabbaticals, encouraging research primarily through promotions policy and, increasingly, in providing some form of in-house training in teaching methods, induction courses for new staff, and courses for middle management.

These activities constitute what is termed 'staff development' in the majority of colleges. The system may work well in those colleges where there has been little change in the role of the teacher and where there has been no significant change of direction or level of work within the college. But staff development in this sense is peripheral to the main work of the college, there is rarely any serious attempt to appraise staff performance and often there is no clear idea of where a department or college is going or what will be demanded of individual staff members in the future. Responsibility for advising and guiding junior staff in their professional activities, for staff development, is given to Heads of Department who themselves have no clear policy framework within which to work. The initiative for attempting to improve on present job performance or to adapt to new methods of teaching remains very much with the individual teacher. There is little direction given by management, and college inservice training units are not seen as central and integral to the work of departments but rather as competitors for limited resources.

Staff development is an institutional response to the developmental needs of both individuals and the college. The teacher requires help in doing his present job more effectively and in adapting to new methods and techniques. For help to be provided requires that deficiencies in the present performance of staff should be identified and that individuals should seek to remedy them. Some form of staff appraisal scheme is necessary and this implies job specification and evaluation. In some colleges, Heads of Department review the performance of their staff annually against agreed targets. Teachers agree with Heads a staff development programme for themselves.

There is also an obligation to prepare the individual teacher for promotion either internal or external to the institution. This requires a college to take a positive stance on its future development, to be explicit about its academic policy and to have a strategy for staff development. Staff development is not an isolated activity — it reflects general pressures and trends. It must be set clearly within a framework of overall institutional development and recognise the pressures and constraints operating upon the college. Staff development must be central to the activity of a college or university and not tacked on as an optional extra!

The Polytechnics have faced the challenge of significant and fundamental change in the short period of time they have had since designation. In the Polytechnics the means of institutional change has been curriculum change and to change and develop the curriculum staff have had to change and develop themselves. Staff development has therefore been central. The Polytechnics were required to submit academic development plans for five years ahead and these plans provided a framework for curriculum and resource development. Their curriculum development has been influenced very much by market demand, by the assumed need of students and the outside world for relevance of study and by the need to innovate and not to compete in the traditional areas with the universities. This demand for relevance has meant greater emphasis in designing the curriculum in operational terms of objectives and process; it has meant the development of multidisciplinary courses rather than single discipline courses as well as a realisation that a continual updating of content and structure of courses is required. The Polytechnics too have involved both consumer (the student) and client (industry and the professions) in the design of their courses. In many cases this involvement has meant more than 'consultation' and far more than asking a few practitioners what they think of a given set of proposals. It has involved academics in meeting together with professionals in other fields to undertake a detailed study of attitudes and skills required in the target group and to plan a satisfactory programme of study. This constant contact with industry and professions through course design and in particular the development of sandwich courses has been a valuable means of staff development as well as securing feedback on course relevance. However, the emphasis on relevance to the student's future career means that the Polytechnics must encourage greater mobility and exchange of staff with the outside world and not rely solely on applied research and consultancy as the means of ensuring that staff keep up-to-date.

Staff development in the Polytechnics has been influenced greatly by the procedures of the Council for National Academic Awards in validating courses. These procedures assume the full involvement in course planning of all staff who are to teach on the course and require from them an understanding of the process of education as well as appropriate subject expertise. The Council's Boards pay particular attention to such things as teaching methods, assessment, the relationships between different parts of a course and the coherence of a student's programme of work. Validating panels include practising professionals who give careful attention to the recent practical experience of staff. Individual staff have been exposed to fundamental questioning by their peers as to their aims in teaching a particular subject on a course. The openness of the course planning process and the opportunity to work things through with colleagues has been of considerable help to inexperienced members of staff. The C. N. A. A. has forced the Polytechnics to take course development very seriously indeed and the validating procedures have led rapidly to a more 'professional' lecturing staff.

The magnitude and the nature of the course planning exercise itself has thrown up all sorts of staff development needs. First of all the switch from Higher National Certificate and Diploma courses with relatively high contact teaching hours and little expectation of independent study to a range of degree courses has forced an investigation into teaching methods and into the use of staff time. This has had considerable implications for the provision of support services — for library services, for administrative and clerical staff backing. Secondly, the stress on relevance has meant that, in recruiting staff from industry and the professions with little teaching experience, the colleges have been required to provide some in-house teacher training. Thirdly, fundamental changes in management style as institutions have developed and changed their role have meant that in-house courses for senior staff have had to be provided. Fourthly, the recruitment of a large proportion of young staff during a period of rapid growth has raised all sorts of problems relating to rapid promotion; and finally the development of multi-disciplinary vocational and innovatory courses with the Polytechnics has caused difficulties for those staff who see their careers as cutting across the binary line, particularly as in many departments junior staff have been required to spend most of their time on course development activities and have tended to neglect their research activities.

The development of the Polytechnics took place during a period of considerable expansion in Higher Education. In particular, the growth of such departments as social science and business and management studies was only possible given the opportunity to 'buy in' a significant number of staff. The likelihood of rapid resource growth once courses had been approved removed from the Polytechnics the urgency of serious institutional planning as distinct from the development of a series of courses related to discernible vocational trends and to staff interests. The problem the colleges now face, given that there will be no additional staff input to fund curriculum change, is to ensure that courses are continually up-dated and that changes reflect the changing external demands likely to be placed on students when graduating. This implies a major role for staff development for there is a danger that courses increasingly will reflect the competencies of existing staff and little change will take place.

Staff development cannot be an isolated activity and it is important that people involved in staff development understand the context and the overall trends and pressures on colleges, and so I want to finish by making some observations about the general climate we find ourselves in today. I make no apology for doing so. It is surprising how many people do not appreciate the change there has been over the last two years. I still hear comments from members of staff in colleges to the effect that '<u>in normal times</u> we would have been able to do this'. It is difficult for college staff to appreciate that we are living in normal times and that the past five or six years have been abnormal.

The first point I would wish to stress is that there is no likelihood of additional resource growth. The 1960s and early 1970s have been abnormal. Even in the early 1970s, since Delaney, staffing has been extremely tight in some areas. In many polytechnics there have been no additional appointments in the science or engineering fields since 1970. Now, however, it is to be right across the board. The Local Authorities generally are discussing cuts in educational expenditure to take effect over the next three years. Higher education will not escape this cut. Change cannot be funded by growth and this inevitably will mean that there will be an emphasis on resource flexibility internally.

The second point is that change will take place. In the public sector our physical resources are planned to accommodate growth and colleges are likely to see a growth in student enrolments on a fixed staffing establishment. The amalgamation of the teacher training colleges with the polytechnics and other colleges requires a shift of resources from teacher training to other areas of work. The continually changing graduate job market also implies curriculum change. Curriculum development has been built in to institutional development.

The third point is that resource reallocation requires hard decisions which will make some people very unhappy. To expand in one area, and to do so without additional resources, requires either greater productivity or a transfer of resources from another area. This implies far more central control over planning decisions — staff do not like making unpleasant decisions which affect their colleagues.

Fourthly, the need for staff redeployment and retraining becomes a priority. This issue is already faced by polytechnics and colleges of higher education who are involved in amalgamations with colleges of education. It is also faced by the schools. If the colleges are to fulfil their obligations and not be forced into creating wholesale redundancy, they need :

1. a realistic appraisal of present staff competencies
2. a realistic plan for institutional development
3. the identification of shortage areas and of over-staffed areas, and
4. proposals for staff retraining.

This requires a substantial change in thought of those responsible for institutional planning, for course approvals (the DES, CNAA, professional bodies) and of the staff themselves.

The ad hoc developments of the past, the luxury of developing the one-off course, just will not do in present circumstances. Some idea of the magnitude of the problem can be gained by taking an example from my own institution where the reduction in teacher training numbers goes from 1300 to approximately 600 over the next three years and this requires the redeployment of some 60 staff.

In many cases redundancy might be an answer, but the obligations on the college are considerable. To make staff redundant requires that you have already done an appraisal of individual staff and that there is little possibility in the college's judgment of any retraining. We do not at present have adequate procedures to cope with this.

Obviously we may expect problems with staff morale because this all violates the understanding on which they have been recruited. Problems of motivation will be caused by a decrease in staff mobility, by the worsening of work conditions and by the encroachment into the minimal discretionary funds at present available to departments. It is tempting for administrators and for local authorities to cut down on such items as staff travel, conferences, visiting lecturers — all the things that make life worth living! We can expect an increase in unionisation, particularly on the non-teaching side. I doubt, too, whether college management is equipped to cope with this.

We need to be far more precise and explicit about resource decisions and the general understanding of the rules of the game. The management problems are particularly acute in the public sector. With large authorities and large colleges, there are problems of delegation and, particularly, there are problems with middle management. If the colleges are to be immune from the arbitrary actions of County Hall and Management Services Department, they have to help themselves and this requires a sophistication of management which we have not yet recognised.

I believe there will be a tendency for far more differentiation between institutions, between departments in the same institution, and between individuals. This will affect staff morale as it will be against staff expectations.

What are the implications of all this? First of all, there will be a significant change in attitude required. Hard thinking needs to be done about institutional planning and redefinition of the role of the teacher. In particular, we need to pay attention to the overlap between the academic and the administrator. Secondly, it requires a sophistication of institutional planning and course planning which we have nowhere nearly researched. Thirdly, it requires an acceptance of change as a fact of life and a systematic review of the work of the college. Finally, it means far more of a central role for staff development, but as an integral part of the institutional planning process. We must learn from the experience of the polytechnics. We must know in far more detail the resource implications of proposals and must look seriously at teaching and learning methods. Staff development activities themselves will be under attack. What, for instance, is the value of a particular course or conference? How do we appraise retraining programmes? What priority is to be given to staff training?

Staff development has become the major vehicle of institutional change. Can we meet the challenge?

STAFF DEVELOPMENT AND RESEARCH ON TEACHING AND LEARNING

by Dai Hounsell, Institute for Research and Development in Post-Compulsory Education, University of Lancaster

One of our main research concerns at Lancaster over the last eighteen months or so has been student learning and development in higher education. We are interested in a number of inter-related questions. How do students go about tackling the complex subject-matter of courses at the higher education level? What styles and strategies do they adopt in learning from reading materials and from lectures and seminars? In what ways do they 'learn' from preparing essays and other assignments? Is it possible to distinguish certain general features of students' intellectual development over the three or four years of an undergraduate degree course? And to what extent, and in what ways, is student learning shaped and modified by the context in which learning takes place — at the level of the course, of the department or faculty, and of the institution?

An attempt to review some of these questions was made in a set of readings published by the Institute some twelve months ago and entitled How Students Learn. More recently, work has begun on a five-year programme of research under the sponsorship of the Social Science Research Council.

My colleagues in this work have backgrounds in psychology and sociology. My own involvement stems from an interest in all aspects of the teaching-learning process and their relevance to staff development. I find it extremely difficult, however, to integrate the findings of research on student learning and development within prevailing modes of thinking about teaching in higher education, for the predominant concern of published work, of staff development activities, and of empirical research has been the impact and relative effectiveness of teaching methods and techniques. Teaching problems have been examined under conventional, everyday headings such as 'lectures', 'seminars', 'practicals' and so on, supported by discussions on 'course development' and 'the use of audio-visual aids'. Teaching success has been seen as dependent on various activities undertaken by the teacher himself, which in turn rest on a core of basic skills which can be inculcated and fostered through induction and in-service programmes of staff development.

This predominant line of approach may be criticised on two grounds. Firstly, it is almost exclusively 'teacher-centred'. Indeed, the widespread use of the term 'the teaching-learning process' seems inappropriate, for the focus of attention has been almost entirely on teaching, with learning viewed at best as a by-product. It seems clear that, whether in undertaking research or staff development, our conceptions of the teaching-learning process have been coloured by our perceptions as teachers. From our particular vantage point, we have viewed teaching in terms of our own, rather limited, immediate concerns; in terms of methods and techniques, of contact hours and formal presentations of subject matter — in terms of the impact of what we as teachers do, without reference to the impact of other significant features of the learning experience as perceived by the student.

Secondly (and this point is related to the first) our conceptualisations of the teaching-learning process have been implicit rather than explicit. There have been few attempts in the literature to articulate models or to develop conceptual frameworks within which teaching and learning might be analysed. Thus innovations have tended to be justified not on pedagogical grounds (i.e. by reference to a thoroughgoing conceptualisation of the teaching-learning process) but rather on grounds which are essentially technological (e.g. 'the systematic use of media promotes more efficient learning') or quasi-ideological (e.g. 'students should be given more autonomy').

Is it possible, then, to articulate a conceptual framework which accords a more significant place to the learner?

Towards a Conceptual Framework

I suggest that we might begin by distinguishing five components, or groups of components. The first four of these are:

the characteristics of the learner: for example, his attitudes and expectations, his previous knowledge and the analytical tools he has acquired, his accustomed modes of tackling subject-matter

the characteristics of the learning task: in terms of, for example, the magnitude of the task, the 'level' and complexity of the subject-matter and necessary 'pre-requisites', the extent to which subject-matter has been (or can be) sequenced and structured

the characteristics of the teacher: such as attitudes and expectations, aims, repertoire of teaching skills and characteristic 'style' of teaching

the characteristics of the environment in which learning takes place: in terms of physical and social setting, of established rules and procedures, mode of operation, implicit norms and values.

The teaching-learning process is thus viewed as a set of interactions between the learner, the learning task or tasks, the teacher, and the learning environment, in relation to a fifth component, time.

The framework makes it possible to discuss the extent to which the characteristics of the learner and the requirements of the learning tasks might be in harmony with one another — to what extent they might be matched or mismatched. We can examine whether this relationship changes over time, as the learner himself develops and the learning task makes new and perhaps more complex demands of him. We can attempt to establish too the likely impact of the learning environment on these relationships — the exigencies of the 'hidden curriculum', for example, the coping ploys that the student may be forced to adopt in order to reconcile the conflicting demands of the different departments which compete for his time and effort. Then there is the teacher himself: he can not only specify the learning task, but make decisions which will determine the 'space of options' for the student: the student's opportunities for exercising choices in relation to subject-matter, for adopting or having to modify his characteristic modes of studying, for relating the content of the learning task to previously acquired knowledge and experience. The teacher may or may not see his 'management of student learning' within a temporal dimension, tailoring the learning task to students' individual needs, and encouraging them (or not encouraging them) to tackle tasks of increasing complexity as they become ready to do so. And lastly, the teacher may shape the learning environment in various ways: through encouraging students to work more closely with their peers, through his own coursework demands, and by the rules and procedures which he establishes or helps establish.

Concluding Comments

The most urgent task for pedagogical research and development in higher education is to develop conceptual frameworks within which the teaching-learning process can be examined and discussed. The analysis of teaching methods and techniques (which has made it possible to provide the neophyte teacher with a range, albeit limited, of tactical options) has served as the foundation stone for staff development; the focus of attention should now shift to a more comprehensive analysis of teaching and learning with an emphasis both on the activities of the learner and on the formulation of strategies for facilitating learning. A corollary of this is the need to re-examine what has come to be called 'staff development'. Perhaps staff development is itself the product of teacher-centred modes of thinking. And shouldn't we then be concerned with the broader concept of 'educational development', and 'develop' the students as learners while we 'develop' the staff as teachers?

Notes and References

ENTWISTLE, N. and HOUNSELL, D. (1976) How students learn (Readings in Higher Education, 1) Lancaster, University of Lancaster, Institute for Post-Compulsory Education

PRINCIPLES UNDERLYING UNIVERSITY TEACHER COURSES

by M.J.A. Mirande, C.O.W.O., University of Amsterdam

I will describe existing and developing practices in the field of university teacher courses. The reason for doing this is to bring about some structure in the great variety of approaches so that the various approaches to university teacher courses may be distinguished more clearly. It is my view that developers of university teacher courses should create a set of different courses to meet the needs of all individual teachers.[1] That's why I am looking for organizational arrangements of and viewpoints to teacher courses, and for principles underlying them.

First I will identify three organizational course arrangements, named the whole, the part and the basis-part approach. Secondly, I will investigate some concepts of teaching and change underlying teacher courses. And thirdly, related to the concepts I point out, I shall deal with four principal views on university teacher courses.

Organizational Arrangements

a) The main characteristics of whole approaches to teacher courses are:[2] groups of teachers attend the course in a fixed sequence and they intend to learn the most important components of the teaching-learning process. One of the advantages of whole approaches is that they offer teachers a related set of insights and corresponding skills. The approach implies that the entire content of the course is of value for every university teacher. The principle is this: everything for everybody.

b) Part approaches start from the principle: something for somebody.[3] They lead to courses consisting of a wide range of short courses; each course has a limited focus and is more or less independent from the other courses. Part approaches lead to more or less individualized formats of instruction.

c) Basis-part approaches seek to combine the advantages of whole and part approaches.[4] A course of this type starts with a short basis-course after which the teacher may choose out of a range of subjects.

Concepts of Teaching and Change

Teacher courses differ on account of their implicitly or explicitly stated underlying concepts of teaching and their concepts of changing behaviour.

a) Analogous to Gage's[5] distinction between passive and active strategies in research on teaching, I discriminate between a passive and an active concept of teaching underlying teacher courses. Courses based on a passive concept of teaching describe teaching as what teachers are doing in the classroom. Courses based on an active concept of teaching describe teaching as bringing about learning situations and seek to supplement the teacher with entirely new models of instruction. Typically, the new model offered by this approach has been based on programmed instruction.[6] The difference between the two approaches may be shortly characterized by 'doing things better' and 'doing better things'.

b) Concepts of change strategy underlying teacher courses differ also. Some courses start very explicitly from an attitudinal concept of change.[7] An attitudinal based teacher course starts from teachers' values, attitudes, assumptions and concerns. Other courses start from some anticipated lack of teachers' technical skill.

<u>Views</u>

Four points of view to teacher courses (see Table 1, p. 14)

a) The Clinic to Improve University Teaching was developed at the University of Massachusetts, Amherst. Teachers requesting assistance from the Clinic work one to one with teaching improvement specialists.[8]

b) Borg[9] and his co-workers at Berkeley's Far West Laboratory for Educational Research and Development are developing mini-courses for commercial purposes. Mini-courses refer to self-instructional workshops or laboratory packages and aim at improving a specific teaching skill.

c) Perlberg[10] describes the Laboratory as a concept of a training system which encompasses a multiple set of activities in which a person is involved individually or in small groups.

d) Gage[11] introduced the concept of the Tools of the Trade. According to him educational research and development should be devoted to the invention, refinement and widespread distribution of tools for teachers and trainers of teachers.

<u>Comments</u>

a) The four principal views put emphasis on four valuable points:

   i. the personal needs of individual teachers (the four approaches are part approaches and lead to more or less individualized formats of instruction);

   ii. the development of technical skills;

   iii. the development of tools for teachers;

   iv. emphasis on both preactive and interactive behaviours of teachers.

TABLE 1: Four points of view to teacher courses, characterized by a concept of change

concept of change / concept of teaching	attitudinal starting from teacher's values, attitudes, assumptions and concerns	technical starting from a lack of skill
passive oriented on classroom performance	the Clinic	the Mini-course
active oriented on bringing about learning situations	the Laboratory	the Tools of the Trade

b) Starting from one approach, e.g. the Tools of the Trade, additional provisions have to be constructed to cope with its shortcomings. At the Centre for Research into Higher Education, University of Amsterdam, a teacher course is being developed of a modular type.[12] This course starts from a programmed part approach, an active concept of teaching and a technical concept of change. The additional provisions are:

i. each module[13] is combined with optional guidance service;

ii. interaction training;

iii. training in the use of audio-visual media;

iv. a mini-library for teachers.

Notes and References

1 cf. PAGE, C.F. (1975) Teasing hamsters in electric cages? Universities Quarterly 29 (3) 318-29

2 For a good example of a whole approach see:
FOSTER, S.F. (1976) The development and preliminary evaluation of a course on improving university teaching performance Submitted papers Second International Conference on Improving University Teaching, Heidelberg

3 For some examples of part approaches see:
SELDIN, P. (1976) Teaching professors how to teach Submitted papers Second International Conference on Improving University Teaching, Heidelberg

4 A Dutch example:
MEER, Q. L. Th. Van Der (1976) Basiscursus onderwijskunde voor docenten Wageningen Bureau Onderzoek van Onderwijs

5 GAGE, N. L. (1972) Teacher effectiveness and teacher education: the search for a scientific basis Palo Alto, Pacific Books

6 cf. GOLDSCHMID, B. and GOLDSCHMID, M. L. (1974) Individualizing instruction in higher education: a review Higher Education 3 (1) 1-24

7 For examples of attitudinal approaches see:
STANTON, C. M. (1976) A perception based model of teacher evaluation Submitted papers Second International Conference on Improving University Teaching, Heidelberg

and

KREME, L. and LIFMAN, M. (1976) University teachers' attitudes and concerns Submitted papers Second International Conference on Improving University Teaching, Heidelberg

8 cf. GOLDHAMMER, R. (1969) Clinical supervision: special methods for the supervision of teachers USA, Holt Rinehart and Winston

9 BORG, W. R., KELLEY, M. L., LANGER, P. and GALL, M. (1970) The mini-course: a microteaching approach to teacher education London, Macmillan
and
PLAS, P. L. and VEENMAN, S. A. M. (1975) De minikursus Pedagogische Studiën 52 (9) 285-95

10 PERLBERG, A. (1976) The use of laboratory systems in improving university teaching Higher Education 5 (2) 135-51

11 GAGE, N. L. (1972)

12 MIRANDE, M. J. A. (1976) De ontwikkeling van een modulaire kursus voor universitaire docenten aan de universiteit van Amsterdam Amsterdam, COWO

13 According to Goldschmid, B. and Goldschmid, M. L. (1974):
"A module is a self-contained unit of a planned series of learning activities which have empirically proven effective in helping students accomplish certain well-defined objectives. Modular instruction, then, may be defined as instruction which is either partly or entirely based on modules."

I am not particularly interested in whether or not Third World people learned sexism from the white man. There have been great cases made to prove how happy men and women were together before the white man made tracks in indigenous soil. This reflects the same mentality of white feminists who claim that all races were in harmony when the "Great Mother" ruled us all. In both cases, history tends to prove different. In either case, the strategy for the elimination of racism and sexism cannot occur through the exclusion of one problem or the other. As the Combahee River Collective, a Black feminist organization, states, women of color experience these oppressions "simultaneously." The only people who can afford not to recognize this are those who do not suffer this multiple oppression.

Moraga, C. (1983). *Loving in the War Years.* Boston: South End Press.

A learning outside the classroom project: Gentle radical activism in solidarity with marginalised communities.

Raising awareness of radical critical thinkers whose work contests patriarchy, racism and capitalism.

To:

From:

Find out more by visiting Tumblr:
https://beneaththealmamater.tumblr.com

20 postcards to be collected, posted on and/or used as a source of strength, critical thinking, solidarity, learning and raised consciousness as a gift for all members of the University community.

6/20

2. STAFF DEVELOPMENT IN THE UNITED KINGDOM (Symposium)

The Nature and Scope of Staff Development in Institutions of Higher Education

Dr. D. Billing (Council for National Academic Awards)

Staff Development and Institutional Change

Dr. R. Cowell (Sunderland Polytechnic)

Staff Development — Policy, Practice and Participation

D. Fox (Trent Polytechnic)

Institutionalization of Staff Development in Higher Education: Observations based on experience at Leicester Polytechnic

J. W. L. Warren (Leicester Polytechnic)

Staff Development in Universities

D. Warren Piper (University Teaching Methods Unit)

Advocates, Acolytes and Adversaries

Dr. C. C. Matheson (University of East Anglia)

THE NATURE AND SCOPE OF STAFF DEVELOPMENT IN INSTITUTIONS OF HIGHER EDUCATION

by Dr. D. E. Billing, Registrar for Science, Council for National Academic Awards

The term 'staff development' has been in common usage now in polytechnics and other higher and further education colleges for at least five years, although it is difficult to trace its history earlier than Tolley's February 1971 paper for the Association of Colleges for Further and Higher Education: as a function of personnel management in industry, the concept has a longer history whence it gains its links with staff appraisal, job description, job satisfaction and career development. Tolley's ideas were taken up in the seminal Association of Colleges for Further and Higher Education and Association of Principals of Technical Institutions joint Working Party report 'Staff Development in Further Education' (London 1973) where the emphasis is again on those aims which derive from the needs of individual members of staff. It is now possible to discern a second major source of staff development aims in the needs generated by the academic plan of the institution and the realisation that staff are a college's major resource. The link with curriculum development was forged in the mid 60's when the CNAA emphasised the importance of staff supporting their honours and postgraduate teaching by ongoing activity in research and consultancy. This requirement was articulated in the Council's 1974 'Report of the Working Party on Resources for Research in Polytechnics and other Colleges', a paper which has been criticised for stretching the meaning of 'research' to the extent where it is almost synonymous with the concept of staff development, which is explicitly mentioned in that report. More recently, sharpening economic pressures and college mergers have given staff development policies a more crucial role to play in utilising given resources so as to enable academic planning goals to be achieved in relation to existing and new courses.

In universities, important landmarks seem to be the 1964 report of the U. G. C. (Hale) Committee on University Teaching Methods, the (Brynmor Jones) report of the Committee on the Use of Audio Visual Aids in Higher Scientific Education (1965), the establishment in 1972 of the Co-ordinating Committee for the Training of University Teachers and perhaps more decisively the 1974 Association of University Teachers/University Authorities Panel Agreement on Probation. This latter document makes it incumbent upon universities to provide training for the probationer and this is having far reaching consequences which may be paralleled in the public sector by the Lecturer Grade II/Senior Lecturer efficiency bar introduced into the 1975 Burnham report (since this implies appraisal), the need to establish criteria for declaring staff redundant and the recommendations on training made by the Advisory Committee on the Supply and Training of Teachers if these are implemented.

It would seem that in universities staff development is seen either as synonymous with staff training methods or as an extension from that base, while in FE staff development often meant simply research, consultancy and industrial/ professional experience and only recently has extended from that base. These origins may reflect the dominance of research in universities and teaching in polytechnics, the development of staff being seen as the provision of opportunities to gain more expertise in the less dominant activities.

The evidence of the replies from 42 of the institutions operating CNAA courses taken with published papers relating to both university and public sector situations points to clear agreement at the general level over what should be encompassed by a definition of staff development: individual and institutional needs should both be recognised as should present and future orientations; programmes to satisfy these needs must resolve any conflicts, should be continuing and should derive from identification and appraisal of needs. The following composite and comprehensive definition is therefore advanced:

> "Staff Development is a deliberate and continuous process involving the identification and discussion of present and anticipated needs of individual staff for furthering their job satisfaction and career prospects and of the institution for supporting its academic work and plans, and the implementation of programmes of staff activities designed for the harmonious satisfaction of those needs."

The scope of staff development activities includes initial and in-service training in educational methods and curriculum development, increasing and up-dating subject knowledge, training in management and committee work, exchange or secondment, study release, research, development and scholarship, creative work, consultancy and professional practice, job rotation, administrative responsibilities, retraining and redeployment of staff, and preparation for retirement.

The major problem seems to be lack of time (i.e. money) coupled with a lack of incentive to undertake work which is not ostensibly related to possible rewards such as promotion. The strong hope that staff development has more to contribute to job enhancement rather than career prospects will not eliminate this latter difficulty. Other problems are the great uncertainty of any academic plan and the hostility of staff to appraisal procedures (apart perhaps from self-evaluation) without which neither of the twin sources of objectives can be identified. Further, conflicts between individual and institutional needs must be resolved and criteria agreed for judging relative priorities, given limited resources.

STAFF DEVELOPMENT AND INSTITUTIONAL CHANGE

by R. Cowell, Dean of Faculty of Humanities, Sunderland Polytechnic

The present context of higher education displays both rapid institutional change and declining projections of student numbers. This combination of circumstances produces difficulties and problems for staff development which were obscured by the rapid expansion of the 1960s. In that decade, the changing demands of higher education institutions were met by the constant influx into higher education of young, highly-qualified and highly-motivated staff. Now, however, the institutional aspects of staff development are less easily met and so staff development programmes must consciously aim to compensate for this decline in the number of new recruits to the higher education profession. However, as well as taking account of this institutional aspect of staff development, any staff development programme must be closely related to actual staff aspirations and priorities.

Sunderland Polytechnic has attempted to reconcile the institutional and individual aspects of staff development by basing its programme on the concept of individual 'profiles' which, while containing certain basic constituents, are sufficiently flexible to incorporate individual needs. These basic constituents, defined on the basis of replies to a preliminary questionnaire to all members of academic staff, are:

(a) Teaching
(b) Research
(c) Consultancy and external contacts
(d) Administration

The underlying assumption of the staff development programme is that every member of staff will make a contribution <u>over a period of several years</u> to all of these aspects of the Institution's needs, but the spectrum of individual emphasis is very wide. The focal point of the staff development programme, in which institutional and individual objectives are reconciled, is the annual 'Staff Development Interview' between each Head of Department and every member of his staff, in which the previous year's work is reviewed and the coming year's work outlined. This is an exchange of views, <u>not</u> a 'staff appraisal' session.

The Department of Education and Science circular 7/73 which has led, in general, to an integration of the teacher education sector into Advanced Further Education, produced at Sunderland in 1974/75 a merger between the polytechnic and the college of education. At an institutional level, the merger was accomplished through the establishment of a new Faculty of Education concerned exclusively with the professional aspects of teacher education and by the absorption of all 'main subject' work into existing and, in some cases, new departments of the polytechnic. This institutional level of the merger provided a solid basis for its staff development programme. However, former college of education staff were faced, in the merger situation, by the necessity of adopting new academic roles and facing new academic challenges, such as CNAA validation. The tensions of this situation are increased by the ever-present possibility of redundancy as the polytechnic teacher education population is reduced by up to 60 per cent. To a lesser extent, established polytechnic staff, both in the polytechnic's former Department of Education and in other departments, are also affected by this influx of staff and, in many cases, have to rethink their career objectives.

Early indications suggest that the staff development programme described above is coping with the problems of the merger precisely because it was designed to take account of, and to reconcile, institutional and individual demands. Inevitably, perhaps, there is a tendency for each academic department to insist that its staff development needs are unique but the flexible 'profile' concept seems, thus far, capable of dealing with specific departmental problems and of finding solutions which contribute to institutional aims. For example, staff 'redeployment' from declining to expanding academic areas can be explored through this system.

As higher education rightly continues to develop new ambitions and structures within a context of slow growth, staff development is inevitably going to be one of the key factors in its success or failure. The system outlined above, still at an early and perhaps crude stage, is basically an attempt to anticipate staff development problems of the late 70s and 80s. It will be monitored annually, to ensure that it does not suffer the fate of many staff development programmes by losing touch with the vital interface between institutional and personal aims.

STAFF DEVELOPMENT — POLICY, PRACTICE AND PARTICIPATION

by Dennis Fox, Staff Development Service, Trent Polytechnic, Nottingham

Staff Development is not something which some people (staff developers) do to others (staff); it is a co-operative exercise in which everyone plays a part — willingly or unwittingly. It is more akin to a system than a process. For this system to be effective, there must be an institutional commitment to staff development and this should be expressed in a declared policy. This policy should be sufficiently non-threatening to be generally acceptable, sufficiently precise to be translatable into action and sufficiently flexible to be opportunist in operation. Staff development is a system for maintaining and increasing the effectiveness of staff — in their present roles and those of the jobs to which they aspire. Effectiveness in this context can be represented by the formula

$$E = e^3 - f$$

indicating that effectiveness is a product of expertise, experience and enthusiasm and it is often reduced by a variety of unintentional and avoidable frustrations. Staff development must address itself to all four of these factors in its concern with increased effectiveness.

It must also take account of the multiplicity of roles performed by academic staff. These are usually identified as teacher, researcher, scholar, counsellor and manager-administrator. No-one working in the polytechnic section with accountants, lawyers, surveyors, planners, engineers, etc. could fail to add the role of professional practitioner. The experience, training and competence in these different roles will vary widely, consequently different groups of staff will have different needs in respect of the different roles. New entrants to the profession come via one or other of two rather dissimilar routes. On the one hand there are the young lecturers who have arrived via a conventional first degree followed by a post-graduate research experience. On the other hand there are those who may not have taken a first degree at all but who have attained full professional qualifications by other means and have entered higher education for the first time, sometimes at fairly senior levels, after extensive experience as practising professionals in industry and commerce. Though both types of new entrant need help with basic teaching skills, they have quite different needs in relation to some of the other roles. The needs of established staff will have a different emphasis. They may be much more confident in their teaching but they may be acquiring administrative and managerial responsibilities for which they have had little preparation and they may be becoming uneasily conscious of their growing remoteness from active professional practice. The complexity of any matrix of needs and roles can be seen from the following diagram:

	Teacher	Researcher	Scholar	Professional	Counsellor	Manager
Young lecturer						
Older Profes-sional						
Estab-lished lecturer						

It would be misleading to put ticks and crosses in the various boxes to represent levels of expertise or degrees of need because most of them would need lengthy elaboration, but the diagram effectively demonstrates the complexity and multi-dimensional nature of staff development. It also highlights the haphazard way in which staff are prepared (or more usually not prepared) for such important parts of their job as teaching, counselling and managing. It is worth noting that only three or four out of the 18 boxes represent roles for which most individuals would claim to be qualified by initial training and recent extensive experience. This is a strange situation, to say the least, for a profession which places such emphasis on qualifications!

A staff development policy should evolve from a consideration of the perceived needs of academic staff in the various roles they have to perform. The role (if any) in this policy of a central unit will vary from institution to institution and hopefully we shall all be able to learn from these different experiences. It will be particularly fruitful to be able to compare the experience of those institutions which have established a strong central unit, perhaps in association with educational technology or curriculum development, with those which see staff development as a more diffuse activity which happens mainly within departments.

Staff development at Trent follows a middle course in this respect and is centred on what might be called intrinsic staff development. This is a recognition that staff, as part of their normal functions as teachers, scholars, researchers etc. are continuously engaged in activities whereby they are seeking to increase their effectiveness in these roles. These activities are concerned with recognising needs, identifying problems and searching for and evaluating solutions. The role of the staff development service is to assist and encourage staff in all these activities. There will probably always be a place in this work for centrally organised short courses and seminars but the most important function is the service provided to departmental or course based study groups and seminars. This ensures that the problems being addressed are the ones which are most closely related to recognised needs.

INSTITUTIONALISATION OF STAFF DEVELOPMENT IN HIGHER EDUCATION: Observations based on experience at Leicester Polytechnic

by J. W. L. Warren, Leicester Polytechnic

Introduction

The following has been suggested by David Billing (Ref 1) as an appropriate definition of Staff Development in Higher Education:

> "Staff Development is a deliberate and continuous process involving the identification and discussion of present and anticipated needs of individual staff for furthering their job satisfaction and career prospects and of the institution for supporting its academic work and plans, and the implementation of programmes of staff activities designed for the harmonious satisfaction of those needs."

As a concept in higher education it has only been in use for some five years. The Joint ACFHE/APTI Working Party Report (Ref 2) on the subject provides a major source of guidance for the formulation of policy and for action at the pragmatic level. At a more idealogical level, D. Warren Piper (Ref 3) writes of the trend towards larger institutions (with accompanying formalisation of procedures and complication of organisation and the need for committee and man management skills), greater accountability for the use of resources (calling for more skill in their allocation), greater accountability to the student body and to bodies outside the teaching institution for what is taught and the standard of teaching, general acceptance that expertise in educational planning and in teaching does not arise from mastery in an academic discipline or a profession, and meaningful probation for tutorial staff.

Many institutions have seen in the concept the need for formal policy and procedures, in short, the need for institutionalisation of staff development. The purpose of this paper is to briefly examine this response to the concept in the light of experience at Leicester Polytechnic.

Formulation of Policy

In 1973 the Academic Body and Governing Body of Leicester Polytechnic decided to establish a number of Assistant Director posts with both Faculty and Polytechnic-wide responsibilities. At that stage the recognition of staff development as a polytechnic-wide responsibility for an assistant director represented no more than an appreciation that in an educational establishment human resources are the major resource and that their conservation and extension is important.

Formulation of acceptable policy in this area depends on wide-ranging consultation thus the Academic Board established a committee in 1974 including the Assistant Director, the Staffing Officer, representatives of Heads of School, academic staff and non-academic staff, and representatives of relevant agencies in the Polytechnic (Research Committee, School of Education, School of Management, Ed Tech Centre, etc.) A policy statement on staff development for academic staff was adopted by the Academic Board on the advice of the Staff Development Committee in July 1975. A summary of the policy is given in the Appendix.

A particular feature of this policy is the Personal Development Programme (PDP) to be established for each member of staff so wishing. The procedure being for each member of staff to receive annually an offer of a Development Discussion from his Head of School, the purpose of which is to establish the PDP. Two points about the procedure should be noted :

i) it is mandatory on the Head of School to make the offer but optional whether the member of staff takes up the offer, and

ii) it is a development discussion not an appraisal interview. Whereas appraisal, if only self-appraisal, is bound to figure in any consideration of desirable development activity, the objective of the discussion is the identification of development activities not the recordings of an appraisal.

The Staff Development Committee proposed this procedure because it was evident that a mandatory appraisal system would not be acceptable to staff and because the real objective in any case was the identification of desirable development activities for the individual.

Another feature of the policy which requires special note is that relating to in-house courses. Although research and participation in conferences etc., taken together are likely to remain the major contribution to the development of staff, co-ordinated in-house courses are seen as making an increasingly important contribution. In particular, it is observed that few academic staff have made a serious study of teaching and learning in higher education or of educational management. The PDP is seen as central to the co-ordination of the provision of such activities on an in-house basis.

Experience with Implementation of Policy

The Induction Course for new staff presented least difficulty organisationally as it was possible to build on some previous experience. It is conducted once every six months for the staff joining the Polytechnic in the preceding period of time and has now been organised on three occasions under the responsibility of the Staff Development Committee. Feedback evaluation of the course has been incorporated as an integral feature and minor modifications have been made on each occasion that the course has been repeated. Although it is mandatory upon Heads of School to release staff to attend, in fact only some 50 per cent of new staff do so, primarily because of the many pressures on their time.

The mandatory initial teacher education courses (the initial teaching methods course and the in-service course of teacher education) are only being organised according to the policy for the first time this session (1976/77) although a less formal activity was organised for new staff last session (1975/76). It is evidently too early to draw any conclusions on the effectiveness of the courses, although some conclusions on organisational matters are becoming apparent, however, the activities organised on an informal basis last session were certainly welcomed by staff.

With regard to the implementation of the policy as it affects established staff the experience with the Development Discussion procedure is the central issue. Anticipating that the formality of the procedure, together with the novelty of such discussions, would present difficulties, meetings were convened in each School to discuss the policy and a short training course was organised by the School of Management for Heads of School. The course for Heads of School consisted of a two hour seminar, to introduce the concepts and procedures, led by expert staff in the personnel management field, followed by videotaped Development Discussion simulations with critical analysis of them. In spite of this preparation only one third of staff across the Polytechnic took advantage of the offer of a discussion in the 1975/76 session, and with large variations from School to School (from zero in one to 85 per cent in another). It is not at all evident why the response to the discussion offer was so low overall, however, a number of factors which might be thought to strongly influence the situation can, in the light of experience, be regarded as secondary. For instance, it might be thought that the attitude and enthusiasm of the Head of School towards the discussion and his/her ability to communicate with staff would encourage participation, but this does not correlate with experience. Further, there is no evidence that either seniority or work load reduces interest in participation or that involvement in major changes in duties or educational developments increases interest. Those approaching the LII/SL efficiency bar appear to be only slightly more interested in development discussions than the rest of their colleagues. However, age particularly proximity to retirement does appear to reduce interest in participation significantly in spite of the Polytechnic's declaration of intent to support personal development activities for those approaching retirement. Research, to date, has not shown staff avoiding participation because they see the procedure as in some way threatening, indeed, such suggestions were rejected at meetings held by Schools. It is tentatively concluded that the attitude to development discussions prevalent in a given School is the major determinant in an individual's perception of the need for a discussion and in whether the offer of a discussion is accepted.

Analysis of the PDPs completed shows, as would be expected, that the most frequently identified development activity is research in the field of the individual's discipline, indeed if broadly defined to cover scholarship, professional practice, consultancy and creative work the majority of staff are so involved. Secondment or exchange has been identified as desirable in seven per cent of cases, for a wide variety of purposes from creative activity in fine art to the production of learning packages through secondment to the Educational Technology Centre. Registration on Masters courses has been identified as desirable for a further four per cent of staff to improve basic qualification, to broaden or to retrain. Registration on in-service courses leading to qualified teacher status is only identified as desirable by two per cent of staff although only some 12 per cent are currently so qualified. However, a full 12 per cent of staff are interested in extending their knowledge of teaching and learning through attendance at in-house workshops and seminars on educational objectives, teaching method (particularly case study methods), AV media and evaluation. Some 10 per cent of staff are seeking development in the general sphere of educational management through in-house courses and attendance at Academic Board and Faculty Board meetings. A further two per cent of staff have been identified as needing a deeper appreciation of organisational objectives. Sundry other in-house activities are identified as of interest to a further five per cent of staff.

Remedial and Re-training Activity

Whereas the staff development policy is concerned primarily with meeting the development needs of the bulk of staff there is also some requirement to remedy deficiencies and retrain.

The introduction of the LII/SL scale and an efficiency bar in 1975 has required the identification of efficiency criteria and the assessment of staff eligible by salary for transfer. The efficiency criteria and the assessment procedure adopted by the Governing Body is quite separate from the development discussion procedure of the Staff Development policy although the advice of the Staff Development Committee was sought. Staff who fail to satisfy the efficiency bar requirements have a development programme devised in discussions involving themselves, a 'friend' (if they so wish), their Head of School and the Assistant Director (Staff Development). Thus far the development needs have divided roughly equally between subject knowledge, teaching ability and other needs. While 100 per cent success cannot be claimed for the development programmes devised in these cases, significant development of staff has been observed both to the benefit of the individual and the Polytechnic.

The merger of the City of Leicester College of Education with the Polytechnic on 1st September 1976 and the cutback in teacher training indicates a retraining requirement. In the area of retraining identification of the institution's academic development plans is crucially important to the identification through discussion of the individual's development programme. Accordingly with the merger so recently effected little progress has been made, as yet, with the identification of retraining programmes. However, experience to date suggests that a combination of teaching team attachment, reading, course attendance (particularly postgraduate courses of the conversion type) and secondment to 'industry' is likely to be fruitful, at least where the member of staff has some relevant scholarship or experience.

There is the risk that too close association of the staff development programme with remedial and retraining activities will result in the bulk of staff associating it with such activities only. It would appear that the only real safeguard against this, at least in the context of established staff, is for resources and opportunities to be widely available and not unduly concentrated on remedial and retraining activities.

Conclusions

The staff development policy and procedures adopted at Leicester Polytechnic effectively institutionalises a process which many might feel should be less structured in order to be truly effective. The formalisation of procedures might be viewed as an organisational response to the demands for greater accountability to government for the use of resources and to the student body and society for what is taught. Formalisation of procedures is not of course necessarily the best response to these demands as staff development is crucially dependent on the active participation of those concerned, which in turn is threatened by over bureaucratic procedures. Indeed, the appropriate response is likely to vary from institution to institution according to the acceptability or otherwise of formal procedures to staff, in which context the acceptability of formal procedures in universities is thought to be low but in polytechnics relatively high.

Formal procedures such as those at Leicester Polytechnic have potentially a number of advantages :

i) new staff join an institution which is known to value teacher education which makes in-service provision for such education and which expects participation,

ii) established staff know that their job satisfaction, both current and future, is recognised to be of major importance and that they have ample opportunity to discuss the matter and develop themselves accordingly,

iii) development needs are identified across the institution so allowing the identification of priorities and the organisation of self-help through in-house courses, changes of responsibility etc., and

iv) divergence between the ambitions of staff and the academic plans of the institution can be identified and dealt with.

The last advantage results from the more explicit nature of the personal and institutional plans associated with the formal procedure and the identification of conflicts at an earlier and usually less difficult stage.

Advantages (iii) and (iv) above depend upon majority participation to have real substance and yet, as reported, only one third of staff participated this session, most probably because the remainder did not perceive sufficient need. This does not imply that these advantages cannot be realised, as one third of staff could accept invitations for development discussions on each year of a three year cycle, and through the long term validity of most personal development programmes effectively constitute 100 per cent participation. Thus only further experience and research will show whether or not the advantages listed will be realised.

The question of whether or not participation would have been greater or less if appraisal interviews rather than development discussions were a feature of the policy is impossible to answer on the evidence available. However, it would appear that neither compulsory appraisal interviews nor compulsory development discussions would be acceptable to staff. Further, it would seem reasonable, in general, to suppose that appraisal interviews would be less popular than development discussions even where both were voluntary, hence the decision to adopt the voluntary development discussions. It will be interesting in due course to compare experience with institutions adopting appraisal interviews as part of a formal procedure.

Although in some ways the initial response to the development discussion opportunity is disappointing, over 100 staff have development opportunities, so identified, available to them this session as a direct consequence of the formal development discussion procedures.

References

1 BILLING, D. E. (1976) Nature and scope of staff development in institutions of higher education SRHE Annual Conference

2 Joint ACFHE/APTI Working Party (1973) Staff development in further education ACFHE

3 WARREN PIPER, D. (1975) 'The Longer Reach' in Issues in Staff Development London SDU/UTMU

STAFF DEVELOPMENT IN UNIVERSITIES

by David Warren Piper, University Teaching Methods Unit, University of London

Implications of Staff Development

The purpose of the paper is to consider some practical implications of introducing staff development schemes into universities. Staff development is defined as: a systematic attempt to harmonize individuals' interests and wishes, and their carefully assessed requirements for furthering their careers with the forthcoming requirements of the organisation within which they are expected to work. Seven practical implications are identified:

1. Individuals should be encouraged to consider and prepare for their future careers
2. Thorough analyses are required of the work undertaken by university staff
3. Staff need time and support to follow development programmes
4. 'Staff development' as a means of changing universities and the acceptance by departmental heads of their management role both need promoting
5. We need to know more about how organisations in higher education work
6. Departments need both the know-how and the means of implementing a staff development scheme
7. Universities require a means of making policy decisions in respect to any conflict of interest which may arise between the career aspirations of individuals and the training needs as seen by their university.

Probationary Staff Training

Three key points in the 1974 Agreement on Probationary Staff Training have practical implications: probationary training must be 'comprehensive'; advice from a senior colleague and attendance at courses should be included; a co-ordinated development programme should last throughout the probationary period. From a close reading of the agreement it can be deduced that 'comprehensive training' means that teaching, research, examining and administration should be covered to the level and in the variety that staff are likely to encounter them in the first six to eight years of their employment. The programme should be sensitive to both the interests of the individual and the likely requirements of his employing institution.

Some Conclusions Drawn

A generalised list of possible training objectives for academic staff may be formulated under the four headings of teaching, research, examining and administration. Advisers will need training; they will need opportunities to meet all together frequently; and their work should be taken into account on consideration of their own promotion. Heads of departments must take responsibility for the development of the staff in their department. Training should be available to assist heads of departments to encompass these duties.

Assessment

Three forms of assessment can be identified: the assessment of work done; the assessment of training needs; and the assessment of an individual's progress. A number of suggestions have been made about the form that reports on junior staff might take.

Information and Resources

There is a continuing requirement for updated information about the staff development activities going on in universities and polytechnics. Institutional staff development units can continue to foster initiatives in the departments, produce training materials, undertake research and development and provide staff training courses. Not only is more money needed for these services but greater imagination is required in how it is spent.

ADVOCATES, ACOLYTES AND ADVERSARIES

by C. C. Matheson, University of East Anglia

There is growing awareness on the part of universities in the United Kingdom of the need to provide continuing support, guidance and training for probationary and experienced university staff. In a few universities the provision of staff development programmes is undertaken by members of staff with full-time responsibility in this area. In most universities, however, such provision is undertaken by individuals, often unpaid and unrecognised, carrying full research, teaching and administrative loads. This paper analyses the background to the current state of staff training and development in terms of the roles taken up, consciously or unconsciously, by individuals and institutions. It is argued that recognition of these roles, and in particular the interplay between them, may assist those who seek to foster staff development in higher education.

Three easily-identified roles are considered in this analysis. First, there are the advocates of training, each with their own set of concepts relating to training. They are seen as carrying the responsibility for the future of training, not only with regard to specifying what traits of staff are to be developed, but also with regard to how the development is to be conducted. Then there are those who anathematise, to a lesser or greater extent, the ideas promulgated by the advocates; these are the adversaries of training. The adversative view may be institutional or individual. Adversaries, perhaps reacting to the missionary-like undertones of the advocates' undertakings, may seek to demote staff development to mere instruction in the elementary skills of lecturing. Finally, there are those at whom staff development programmes are directed — the acolytes. Probationers have acolyteship thrust mandatorily upon them, institutionally by their universities and personally by the advocates within their universities. Acolyteship is a role which, to the regret of advocates, too few senior academic staff seem anxious to assume formally.

These three roles, advocate, acolyte and adversary, are not mutually exclusive; nor indeed is it always possible to foresee, control or change the role adopted by particular individuals or institutions. Thus a probationer, rather than becoming a neophyte advocate, may as a result of his experience of training, join the ranks of the adversaries.

It is argued that the particular role adopted by an individual vis-à-vis training reflects the total experience of that individual. In that sense the adopted role is a reality for that individual. There is, therefore, a real conflict of view between those in the opposing roles of advocate and adversary. This is somewhat analogous to the conflict between an earth-bound scientist expressing his observation of a physical law: 'What goes up must come down', and an astronaut in conditions of zero gravity expressing his observation of the same law: 'What's put stays put'. In this case the conflict may be resolved by either observer amending his ideas to take account of the physical circumstances of the other. Only by means of such transformation of ideas are the apparently conflicting observations seen as different but equally valid statements of the same universal law of physics. A parallel can be drawn between such a transformation, which relates different experiences of the same physical law, and the process which is necessary to reconcile different experiences of staff training. It is suggested that the responsibility for reconciliation between advocate and adversary lies with those who adopt the advocative role. Thus the advocate should strive to frame his detailed proposals for training in ways that are acceptable in the adversary's experience while still preserving the fundamental principles of training as derived from his own experience. This, of course, implies that the expert in training has to examine, learn about and acknowledge the validity of the attitudes of others towards his specialized view of the world.

This analysis provides a perspective from which to view, for example, current efforts being made by universities to implement the agreement between the University Authority Panel and the AUT on the procedure and criteria to be used in connection with the probationary period.

3. STAFF DEVELOPMENT IN OTHER COUNTRIES

The Doctor of Arts: a New Degree for College Teachers

Professor P. L. Dressel (Michigan State University)

Improving University Teaching through Staff Development Programs

Dr. D. Brandt (Centre for Research into Higher Education, Technische Hochschule, Aachen)

Professional Training and Development of Academic and Administrative Staff in Higher Education

Dr. J. Clark (Melbourne State College)

THE DOCTOR OF ARTS: A NEW DEGREE FOR COLLEGE TEACHERS

by Paul L. Dressel, Michigan State University

Why a New Doctoral Degree?

Concern about college teaching is not new, but recent trends have reinforced it The trends include: a marked increase in student numbers during the period, 1940-1970, a shift in enrolments from small private colleges to large public universities and community colleges, and student insistence that instruction be relevant to life and work. The research-oriented Ph. D., with its assumptions that research activity is essential to good teaching and that good teaching is little more than presenting a discipline in its purest form to students, has long been considered a useful way of certifying faculty competency, but is largely irrelevant for undergraduate college teaching.

In a few universities, recognition of these deficiencies led to programme adjustments permitting the inclusion of experiences relevant to teaching, but the majority of graduate faculty members have regarded such adjustments as destructive of the quality and character of the Ph. D. The preferred alternative has been to develop a new degree different in nature and purpose from the Ph. D., called the Doctor of Arts (D. A.) Unfortunately widespread insistence that the new degree be equal in rigour and respectability to the Ph. D., has led too frequently to the perpetuation of largely irrelevant Ph. D. requirements, such as competence in foreign languages or research.

American higher education requires that every undergraduate should be liberally educated through study of disciplines other than his major. Now, instruction that is acceptable for majors may be totally inadequate for weakly motivated non-majors, and many colleges have attempted to meet the breadth requirement by broad interdisciplinary courses for which the single discipline doctorate is inadequate preparation. Thus both instructional competencies <u>and</u> content had to be addressed in planning D. A's.

Programmes for the Doctor of Arts

In spite of the fact that D. A. programmes were started in an adverse economic climate, they now exist in over 25 universities and numerous disciplines (English, mathematics, chemistry, biology, economics, physics, history, German, psychology, political science, art, music, medical technology, library science). The range of institutions extends from such widely known and highly regarded ones as the University of Michigan, Carnegie-Mellon University, University of Washington, Lehigh University, and the University of Mississippi to regional universities not previously involved in doctoral programmes. Several of the universities already offered the Ph. D. and introduced the D. A. as an alternative. Other universities undertook to develop the D. A. as the first and only doctoral programme. Inevitably, the interpretation of the Doctor of Arts degree has varied markedly. The requirements have depended upon the views of faculty members, many of whom still regard the Ph. D. as the best preparation for teaching. Some D. A. programmes have differed from the Ph. D. only in permitting research of a practical turn. Generally, however, most D. A. programmes contain the following components :

a) A broad rather than specialised treatment of the discipline.

b) One or more courses or seminars on such topics as teaching methods, curriculum development, higher education, history, educational philosophy, evaluation, psychology, and governance. These may be existing education or psychology courses, seminars within the student's department or special seminars under the auspices of the graduate office set up for all D. A. students. The latter approach is preferred by those that believe some of the most significant issues about curriculum and teaching transcend the disciplines.

c) Supervised classroom teaching, either within the university or in an undergraduate college. Supervision of an externship poses some difficulties and the extern must adapt rather than innovate. My own conviction is that unless the university can provide a teaching internship on its own campus, the university should not offer the Doctor of Arts degree. Some universities and some departments have waived the internship for persons with several years of experience, but have instead required students to take additional substantive courses in their discipline.

d) A scholarly product variously designated as a research project, a thesis, or a dissertation usually, but not always, having some relevance to teaching. Examples include development of new course material, evaluation of a new course, preparation of new materials for an existing course, and a review of research which suggests a new approach or a new mode of teaching. Some departments prefer the Ph. D. type of dissertation, but require that it be accompanied by a final chapter discussing consideration of the implications of it for undergraduate teaching. A few departments specify two half dissertations: one research-oriented, the other dealing with a teaching problem. In a few D. A. programmes, faculties, in their concern that a research dissertation not be required, have come close to specifying the D. A. as a degree in which there is no culminating piece of scholarship. This should be resisted.

e) Courses in disciplines related to the major field — a recognition that many undergraduate courses are problem-oriented or interdisciplinary in nature.

f) Skill courses in statistics, tests and measurements, or other fields. A few programmes require foreign languages, largely to maintain Ph. D. standards. Others would impose some skill in the use of educational technology. There are marked differences of opinion in this area and consequent differences in requirements.

g) Examination requirements which tend to parallel those for the Ph. D., although the relevance of some of the preliminary, core, or comprehensive examinations required by some departments for the Ph. D. is uncertain. A few departments have no final oral examination, although the merits of this (judging from my interviews) as a final culminating episode for a doctorate seem to be accepted by most professors and doctoral students.

Models for College Teaching

There is not, and there is not likely to be, accord upon the characteristics of a good college teacher. Disciplines differ significantly. Some, such as mathematics and the natural sciences, are highly cumulative in nature and require intensive and protracted study over a period of time. Individuals who go into these fields are apt to differ in many ways from persons who go into the social sciences and humanities. For example, they are more likely to be interested in things and in abstractions rather than in people and in social interactions. There are also differences among students who go into the various specialties. Undoubtedly one of the reasons why there is so much complaint about teaching in mathematics is because students whose primary interests are in other areas are increasingly required to acquire a degree of facility in mathematics, although they view it as merely a tool which they would like to acquire as quickly and as painlessly as possible. Among students also there is considerable variation in ability, differences in interests, attitudes and cognitive traits, and certainly marked differences in career orientation. All of these factors interact with the nature of the discipline and the characteristics of the teacher. To these variables could be added many others dealing with the college environment, with the nature of the programmes available in the college, and with the traditions and purposes of the institution.

In the single disciplinary emphasis, still characteristic of many English universities, the professor may well be a person whose primary interest is in his discipline and in those students who share his interest in that discipline. Many of his students may also desire to attain a high level of competence in that discipline and see him as a model which they wish to emulate. Such a professor is not likely to find much satisfaction in teaching in an American community-junior college nor are the students likely to find him a very good teacher. Most of his students will have no great interest in the discipline, whereas his primary concern is with the discipline and the expansion of the discipline rather than in the interpretation of the discipline to those who are not especially interested in it. Such a professor may be an excellent teacher in graduate schools or even in a liberal arts college where there are exceptionally good students majoring in his field who plan to go on for graduate study.

Some professors (our second type) achieve a reputation simply because they are interesting personalities who interact well with students. Some of these may have an orientation to social problems or the problems of young people rather than to their discipline, which make them particularly attractive as instructors for students who are also oriented to these problems. At best, such teachers incite students to high standards of performance, at worst, they become mere entertainers. Nevertheless, when the full range of educational objectives is taken into account, such a professor may make an outstanding contribution to the development of individual students.

A third type of professor finds his discipline his major concern, but sees his primary challenge as the interpretation or communication of that discipline to others. It is this type of professor who becomes particularly concerned about his teaching methodology and his materials, who becomes concerned about evaluating the impact of his course upon students. With this type of professor, emphasis shifts from the teaching act to the student learning which ensues from it. Such a professor may have almost sole concern with cognitive objectives and the extent to which his students achieve them, although the fact that he is concerned with what his students learn and how much they learn, will in the best induce an awareness of emotional or affective factors which condition or which emanate from learning.

A fourth type of professor is one especially concerned with affective outcomes. Such professors are more likely to be found in the humanities, social sciences, and the arts than they are in mathematics and the natural sciences. The disciplines in the humanities, social sciences, and the arts are much closer to the values, the feelings, and the attitudes of people. Certainly one does not achieve any high level of mastery in these disciplines unless there is a sensitivity to values and feelings. In the extreme, such a professor may completely discount the significance of the discipline in which he has been trained and the principles, concepts, and structure of that field as providing learning outcomes for his students. Thus some experimental programmes at the undergraduate level have become a combination of free expression and group therapy, defended on the ground that this leads to self-insight, self-understanding, personal growth and development, and increased ability in interacting with others. For my own part, I believe that this orientation to affective outcomes to the exclusion of some increased intellectual ability based upon organised knowledge is a complete misconception of the education process. While I have no difficulty in accepting this approach as a constructive therapeutic exercise for which individuals might well pay as much or more than they pay for tuition and fees in a college, teachers and administrators who permit such a pattern in a college may well be criticised for extracting money under false pretences.

One might regard the Type 1 professor as little concerned with affective outcomes and dealing with values only indirectly as these are intrinsic to the materials which he presents. The Type 2 professor, in contrast, may have values which extend well beyond his discipline but his attention to values is indirect and his impact on students problematic. The professor of the third type accepts as his primary value the development of individuals to the point where they have some insight into the discipline and some ability to use it. This professor may, at times, even compromise or ignore certain of the values implicit in the discipline. The fourth type of teacher is likely to insist that students differ markedly in their attitudes and values and that his only concern as a teacher is with regard to affective outcomes.

In presenting the preceding types, it is not my intent to say that one type of teacher is necessarily better than another or that every teacher can be clearly categorised. Rather, the point is that there are different models of good teaching; that these models may be appropriate in various circumstances depending upon the students, the discipline, the capabilities and commitments of the professor, and the purposes of the institution. It should also be apparent that as a prospective teacher becomes sensitive to the differences in the differences in these models and undertakes to prepare specifically to become a particular type of teacher, the experiences which are appropriate may differ markedly. Whereas the traditional Ph. D. may well be the best type of preparation for Model 1 and perhaps almost equally good for Model 2, it is certainly not appropriate for Model 3, and may be entirely irrelevant for Model 4. Indeed, in my observation, many of the professors fitting into Model 4 (in the extreme position of commitment to affective outcomes) have either not finished a doctorate or have been antagonised by the experience and, in part, have moved to their present position by their reaction against their own past education.

Conclusion

The Ph. D. has, in theory if not always in practice, a sequential cumulative quality starting from an overview of a discipline based upon undergraduate and early graduate study and gradually narrowing down to a subfield for more intensive study. The programme is capped by a piece of research acceptable to scholars in that discipline. The Doctor of Arts degree is a professional degree requiring high level competence in the discipline, but focusing on communication of that discipline to non-specialists concerned with applications rather than with the discipline itself. Proponents of the D. A. insist that good teachers must be informed about learning and skilful in using learning resources to motivate and increase student learning. Although few good models exist, the majority of the D. A. candidates to date have had several years of experience and have been deeply interested in teaching. Some have known far more about the complications of teaching than their Ph.D. professors. Such students assure a good product!

Ultimately, the D. A. programme should encourage the candidate to define from his prior teaching experiences a course or aspect of a course which requires improvement. He will begin by defining its objectives, explore available instructional materials, develop new materials, and plan for evaluation. At some point, all are brought together in a teaching experience more profound than any prior one, to be observed and evaluated by qualified teachers. Finally the candidate reports his work in the form of a dissertation. In this sense, the D. A.

experience could have a sequential, cumulating, unifying quality which is presently lacking.

An additional factor largely absent from most D. A. programmes concerns the interrelationship of a discipline with other relevant fields of study; for example, the relationship of mathematics to business, engineering or social science. There is an awareness of this need in some of the D. A. departments and a few have developed courses to meet the need, but most departments tend to view the D. A. (like the Ph. D.) as a single discipline degree.

It may be appropriate to end on a personal note. As one who has looked closely at the D. A., I am sometimes viewed as a proponent for it and as having a stake in its future. In fact, my own concern has been with the improvement of college teaching, and my personal belief is that the Ph. D. could and should have been modified to include experiences preparing for teaching. A few universities have done this. I do not think that a second degree was necessary, and it has been forced upon us only by the views of those scholars who regard teaching as a subsidiary task to research. These views still exist and, because of them, D. A. programmes will continue.

References

1 DRESSEL, Paul L. and DELISLE, Frances H. (1972) Blueprint for Change: Doctoral Programs for College Teachers Iowa City, Iowa American College Testing Program, Monograph Eight

2 DRESSEL, Paul L. and THOMPSON, Mary Magdala (1974) College Teaching: Improvement by Degrees Iowa City, Iowa American College Testing Program, Monograph Thirteen

IMPROVING UNIVERSITY TEACHING THROUGH STAFF DEVELOPMENT PROGRAMS

by Dr. D. Brandt, Centre for Research into Higher Education ('HDZ'), Technische Hochschule (RWTH) Aachen, West Germany

The Centre for Research into Higher Education (HDZ) at the Technische Hochschule (RWTH) Aachen was established in 1974. Its main tasks have emerged as the offering of courses to improve university teaching. The aims of such courses are:

a) to make obvious to the participants problems of university education

b) to develop and practice techniques of presenting material

c) to foster an awareness of the various ways in which lecturers and students may interact

d) to allow the participants to try out or to practice specific methods of teaching which may be considered alternatives to the usual behaviour in classrooms

e) to bring about change in the structure of student-staff communication, toward a more symmetrical process of teaching where both teacher and students think of themselves as being learners

f) to stimulate as well as encourage the participants to support innovations and reforms in university teaching.

The HDZ Aachen has been involved in implementing three different approaches to improving university teaching through staff development:

a) The HDZ itself offers formal courses to junior staff members of engineering departments of the Technische Hochschule (RWTH) Aachen. An interdisciplinary project team of research students assists in running these courses comprising students of physics, engineering, education and social sciences. The courses last about eight weeks during term time, with two – four hours a week.

b) At the University of Bochum (about 200 km from Aachen) a working party was established in 1974, by the Vice-Chancellor of the university. It comprises professors and junior staff members of mathematics, science, literature, medicine, psychology from both the University of Bochum and the HDZ Aachen. The working party has implemented courses on teaching methods offered to staff members throughout the University of Bochum. The pattern of these courses are:

i) a three-day residential workshop for about 40 participants, as an introduction to various aspects of university teaching

ii) another three-day residential workshop on feedback and examination problems

iii) a follow-up working group for one semester

iv) a one-semester working group which aims at improving the participants' teaching behaviour

c) The University of Bochum, in collaboration with the HDZ Aachen, and the I. E. T., University of Surrey, has established an interdisciplinary project team comprising staff members of the three institutions involved. This team offered a four-days residential workshop for university teachers in September 1976. It was the first workshop on staff development to be offered to academic staff in West Germany as a whole; according to feedback from participants, the course was well received. Similar ones are planned by the same team, for 1977.

PROFESSIONAL TRAINING AND DEVELOPMENT OF ACADEMIC AND ADMINISTRATIVE STAFF IN HIGHER EDUCATION: THE ROLE OF A FORMAL PROGRAM OF STUDY IN EDUCATION

by Jean Clark, Department of Physics, Melbourne State College

The Diploma of Education Course

In 1971 Monash University Higher Education Research Unit (HERU) presented a part-time diploma of education course specifically designed for staff of tertiary institutions. A high percentage of places were reserved for staff of Monash University and the table below gives the student population of the initial intake.

STUDENTS		DISCIPLINE AREA	
Monash University	12	Science/Engineering	12
Colleges of Technology	5	Economics/Psychology	3
Teacher Training Colleges	2	Arts/Languages	4
Other	2	Other	2

The course started with a meeting of the students and staff, followed by an intensive period of eight evenings, spread over two working weeks. Each evening lasted from about 4 -11 p. m., with a break of about an hour for dinner where staff and students ate together in the university staff club. Thereafter the course was conducted formally for one evening per week, during regular term time, over two years, each evening lasting from about 5 -10 p. m., with a break for dinner. The topics studied were as follows :

Unit 1	Semester 1 and 2	1971	'Methods and Practice of Teaching
Unit 2	Semester 1	1972	'Institutions of Tertiary Education'
Unit 3	Semester 1	1972	'Students in Tertiary Institutions'

In the first unit structure was imposed by a fairly formal session, led by members of HERU during the first part of the evening. After dinner the format varied between formal student presentations, small group sessions with a report back function, discussion groups or project group sessions. At some stage during the year all students were visited by a member of HERU staff who sat in on a lecture or tutorial given by the student in his/her home institution. The second and third units were presented by members of Monash University Education Faculty. In the second unit a degree of structure was maintained with staff members taking lead sessions, but with student led sessions frequently occurring. In the third unit nearly all sessions were student conducted.

The pre-course meeting and the intensive initial sessions welded the participants into a group, and social and professional contacts have endured over the period of time since the course finished. The degree of involvement of the HERU staff was an essential and obvious ingredient. For me the most profound change that occurred was a realisation of the essential inter-relationship between teaching and learning. I came away from the course far less confident that I knew 'the answers'. I had however learned to ask a lot of questions.

Staff Development and Advancement

Graduates from the first three intakes were given questionnaires and interviews and responses from 46 participants were obtained, including two above Senior Lecturer, six Senior Lecturers, 32 Lecturers and six below Lecturer.

It appears that in terms of staff development the course has been an overwhelming success. The majority of graduates feel that they are now:

a) more confident in their role as educator/teacher (67%)

b) more aware of student needs in the learning situation (78%)

c) questioning their own courses (87%)

d) considering objectives for their courses (91%)

e) changing their teaching methods (83%)

Many graduates have written teaching programmes, introduced different assessment procedures, produced AVA material, initiated course design and evaluation projects and have become members of institution and state-wide committees on teaching and learning. Many have presented papers on their innovations at seminars and conferences and have had journal articles published.

Most students enrolling in the course did not do so to improve their promotion prospects and only 20 per cent say it may have helped in gaining promotion. Half claim there has been an increased interest and satisfaction in their job, but several said that their interest has decreased. However, more disturbing than the statistical data are comments relating to conflict, all of which indicate a deep division between the personal aims and commitment to teaching and the institutional positive recognition only of academic research.

Conclusions

Nearly all tertiary institutions claim that excellence as a teacher is a prime requirement of staff members, and yet it appears that when staff take this claim seriously and widen and deepen their experience in this area it has little effect on their careers. Most graduates in the Diploma of Education course have documented evidence which shows their interest in, and professional acceptance as good teachers; evidence which is very similar to that accepted as a measure of a good researcher (thesis, publications, membership of professional societies, committee membership, research grants). If tertiary institutions continue to claim that they require staff to undertake teaching, research and administrative duties then it would seem appropriate that all three should be accorded respect. It would appear that while staff development will continue as legitimate and necessary, in the future much greater attention must be given to institutional development, especially the development of an attitude within an institution that does not belie its stated aims.

4. STAFF PERCEPTION OF THEIR ROLE

TEACHER OPINION ON POSSIBLE CRITERIA FOR THE ASSESSMENT OF ABILITY IN TEACHING AND LECTURING

by P. A. Ongley, University of Aston

Recently the 450 full-time teachers at the University of Aston were asked to answer a questionnaire on possible criteria of ability in teaching and lecturing. Although only 134 (29%) responded, the results were probably free from statistical bias. Respondents were asked to assess items on a 0-to-5 scale (0 – unimportant, 5 – very important), (a) for confirmation of tenure (satisfactory completion of probation), and (b) for promotion to Reader/Senior Lecturer. It will be seen that with the exception of items 9 and 11, which is not unexpected, there are no significant differences between (a) and (b). These results would therefore suggest that academics consider that the same criteria for good teaching should be used when judging young and experienced teachers.

TABLE 1

	Items of possible relevance in assessment of teaching	(a) For tenure	(b) For promotion
1.	Work recently taught (up to 5 years)	3.0	3.7
2.	Lecturing ability, as assessed by a colleague	3.5	3.4
3.	Use of handouts	2.0	2.0
4.	Teaching results (success of students)	3.1	3.2
5.	Attitude to class and teaching	4.4	4.4
6.	Attitude to students	4.5	4.3
7.	Use of student feedback	3.4	3.6
8.	Willingness to learn of new education developments	3.4	3.6
9.	Textbooks written	1.1	2.9
10.	Published papers on educational topics	1.7	2.3

/contd.

TABLE 1 (contd.)

Items of possible relevance in assessment of teaching	(a) For tenure	(b) For promotion
11. Contributions to curricular development or committees in or out of the university	2.0	2.3
Items on how an observer can assess lecturing ability (see 2 above)		
12. Oral presentation	4.1	4.1
13. Boardwork and/or overhead projector	3.5	3.2
14. Use of audio-visual aids	2.6	2.6
15. Use of handouts	2.4	2.4
16. Suitability of subject matter (level and syllabus)	4.4	4.4
17. Control of and relationship with class	4.1	4.3

(In all cases the standard deviation is between 1.0 and 1.5)

AN EXPLORATORY STUDY OF THE PROFESSIONAL SOCIALIZATION OF UNIVERSITY TEACHERS

by R. J. D. Rutherford and P. H. Taylor, University of Birmingham

Professional socialization is the process by which a person becomes a fully fledged member of a profession entitled to all the courtesies and privileges attendant on achieved professional standing. It is to study this process as it applies to the profession of university teachers that the research project to be reported here was embarked upon. It has taken as its initial sample all staff in one university who are new to university teaching. The methodology employed is that of the guided interview based on a preliminary questionnaire. Staff were invited to outline their reasons for embarking on a university career, their expectations of the job before being appointed, and how these had worked out in practice. They were also asked to comment on their own immediate satisfactions and disappointments with university life, and on how they expected their career to develop. The role of the department in the crucial first few months of a new lecturer's career was probed, in terms of the demands made on new staff for teaching, examining, administration and research, and also the extent to which such functions, especially those associated with teaching, were discussed in the department. The interviews were recorded and constitute the data of this study. Currently only an exploratory analysis of the findings can be offered.

In a very preliminary way the data we have suggests that the process of professional socialization undergone by university teachers appears to possess the following characteristics:

a) <u>It is highly informal</u>

None of the departments had formal means for the induction of new members into their professional role over and above the specification of his teaching and other duties. No evidence has been found of departments providing 'training for the probationer of a helpful and comprehensive nature' or 'a co-ordinated development programme which lasts throughout their probationary period' as indicated in the UAP/AUT Agreement on Probation. On the contrary staff refer again and again to being 'thrown in at the deep end'. However this situation does not seem to be completely unwelcome to the majority of staff. They value their independence and freedom of action, indeed this seems to be one of the main reasons for embarking on a university career. A common reaction is 'I don't want people interfering'.

b) It is assumed from the outset by members of a department that the newcomer is a colleague of comparable standing

This confers on the newcomer immediate equality of status. He becomes fully fledged from the start with little to learn but his way around the department, its hierarchy and its way of doing things. It follows that to describe the newcomer as an acolyte (an attendant, a candidate) is inappropriate. Moreover the suggestion of serving an apprenticeship and being offered 'advice and guidance by a senior colleague nominated for this task', as recommended in the Agreement on Probation, met with a cool response. On more than one occasion feelings ran high. 'I don't think I would have come under those circumstances anyway. I would have been upset if I thought I was going to be spoon-fed. I have to sort it out for myself, I am no puppet-on-a-string'. Staff appear to prefer to consult a colleague whom they know and respect and who would have knowledge and experience of the particular problem in hand. In one department, where promotion depends very much on the amount of administrative responsibilities, it was suggested that 'it would be another job to be collected'.

c) It holds few surprises

Although the amount of administrative work and time required to prepare for lectures and seminars is sometimes greater than expected, for the most part no differences were found between how new staff imagined the job to be and what turned out in practice. This is hardly surprising, as most of the staff interviewed were in their mid-twenties and had spent their previous years in university life. The description of a new member of staff as a neophyte (one who is newly initiated) is therefore most misleading. For many, a university career is 'what I've always wanted'. Possibly their attitude to 'training' is conditioned by this knowledge of what is entailed in a university teacher's job?

d) It is rooted in subject competence rather than in teaching abilities

Staff from disciplines as varied as law, chemistry and history emphasised that they had developed their own personal approach to the subject and this was what they hoped to communicate to their students. Scholarship and research potential are the major attributes on which appointments are made, and on appointment become the basis for the ready conferment of largely achieved professional status on the newcomer.

e) It leads to a lack of balance between subject competence and teaching ability

An overwhelming impression was gained from the interview that these staff were both keenly interested in teaching and very much aware of their responsibilities to students. However it was also clear that they are placed under no obligation by their departments either to improve their competencies as teachers or their sensitivities as personal tutors. In the departments the concepts of the university as a place of learning and of the staff themselves as learners are generally more highly regarded than that of the university as a teaching institution, and staff respond accordingly.

The implications of this exploratory study are tentative. But it may be that the UAP/AUT Agreement on Probation, especially Paragraph Four, stands little chance of acceptance, either by departments (because it represents such a radical departure from current practice) or by new staff (to whom the notion of 'training' with its implication of lack of competence is anathema). It may indeed be the case that the Agreement, with its emphasis on formal courses and supervision, may be a hindrance to staff development at the present time.

A FIRST STEP IN STAFF DEVELOPMENT: SECURING BASELINE DATA ON TEACHING PRACTICE

by D. M. Rhodes, Illinois State University

Introduction

Baseline data for staff development purposes include information about staff and student characteristics, organizational structures and support services, and the status of teaching practice. Such data can be used to describe the institutional context with respect to instruction at the time a staff development programme is being proposed or established. This paper is confined to the rationale and methods for, and problems related to, acquiring baseline data on teaching practice, and will be illustrated by procedures now being used or planned in the W.K. Kellogg Project Teaching-Learning Center at Illinois State University.

Baseline data on teaching practice are information about the teaching procedures actually being used in an institution, the quality of these procedures as carried out, the perceptions students and staff have concerning teaching at that institution, and the attitudes they display toward it. They should not be confused with an approach more common in staff development, known as 'needs assessment', where staff members are asked what developmental activities they 'need'.[1]

Baseline data will not, for instance, supply relevant value criteria to be used in deciding whether or not staff should be trained. They do, however, constitute the basic information to which the criteria may be applied to make that determination. Without them, it is difficult to make decisions about staff development on any but ideological grounds. If staff development is to become more than another trendy fad, it must be grounded in substantive data.

Within the staff development process itself, there are at least three stages at which baseline data are required. First, when a developmental programme is being proposed, second when it is being implemented, and third, when it is being evaluated.

Establishing Baseline Data

At present the collection of these data must be done on an institutional basis because, as yet, there is not enough evidence to conclude that the data are generalizable from one institution to another. Given the wide range of possible institutional aims and responsibilities, there is little reason to believe that similar conditions will hold throughout higher education. Individual universities, polytechnics, and colleges can be expected to differ in the emphasis they place upon teaching and in the quality of the teaching practised. It might be claimed that certain procedures, such as the lecture, are universal, but there is no evidence that staff satisfaction with, or student response to, lectures is for example the same in England as it is in the United States.

It might be argued that while institutions may differ, there are indeed certain 'competencies' which everyone performing the function of teacher in higher education must have. Unfortunately for those who hold this position, research has not discovered any 'indispensable teaching behaviours' which all staff might be expected to acquire.[2]

Though baseline data are necessary, there are at present no adequate theoretical grounds for determining what aspects of teaching practice are most significant for staff development purposes, and which should therefore be emphasised in the data-gathering process. In the absence of such a theoretical formulation, the kinds of baseline data which should be collected would seem to be those sufficiently basic and general that their value may be assumed. These include information on: (1) actual teaching practices; (2) attitudes toward teaching held by students and staff; (3) quality of teaching practice in terms of proximity to performance models; and (4) problem areas in teaching as defined by students and staff. Data on teaching practices include type and frequency of expressed goals (e.g. intellectual development, vocational preparation), types of programme contexts (e.g. general education, postgraduate instruction), type and frequency of teaching procedures used (e.g. lectures, computer-assisted instruction), and the types of support services and degree to which they are utilized (e.g. television, library).

Information on attitudes toward teaching held by students and staff should include both the degree and the source of satisfaction or dissatisfaction with teaching practice as described above. Quality of teaching practice should be determined with respect both to the proficiency with which the teaching procedures are carried out and to the sophistication of the activities intended by the instructor and undertaken by the students. Problem areas as defined by students and staff are less easily categorised, but should fall into the general areas of staff competence (e.g. use of teaching procedures, subject knowledge), student capabilities (e.g. motivation or lack of it, range of abilities), institutional climate (e.g. rewards for teaching, attitudes toward publication), administrative arrangements (e.g. quality of physical facilities, number of contact hours), and support services (e.g. availability, co-operation of staff).

Experience at Illinois State University

To collect these data, a number of procedures are being used and/or developed by the Kellogg Project Teaching-Learning Center at Illinois State University. These include survey instruments, interviews, small group meetings using problem identification techniques, personal inquiries to the Center, and institutionalised student/peer/administrator evaluations used for promotion, tenure, and merit-salary decisions. One of the first problems facing anyone who wishes to collect data on teaching practice is the lack of materials specifically designed for that task. For this reason, we in the Teaching-Learning Center are utilising currently available instruments where possible and devising others when necessary.

To obtain generalised information about teaching aims, we have been able to use results from the Institutional Goals Inventory (IGI).[3] The IGI has been developed by the Educational Testing Service; it was administered through the Office of Undergraduate Instruction to some 500 staff members (among others) in 1975. This inventory provides information about staff perception of 'outcome' and 'process' goals and reveals discrepancies between the staff perceptions of what 'is' and what 'should be' on topics such as intellectual orientation and vocational preparation.

In surveying the literature on staff development we have been unable to locate suitable instruments for gathering data on actual teaching practices as carried on by instructors or staff attitudes about teaching, so we have devised two of our own for this purpose. These are the 'Teaching Practice Interview' and the 'Teaching Practice Survey'. The Teaching Practice Interview is a 20-item interview schedule which is designed to be administered to staff members on an individual basis. It includes questions on such topics as teaching experience, class size, programme contexts, aims, colleagues' competence in teaching, and support services. These questions allow staff members to describe the teaching they do, to express satisfaction or dissatisfaction with various aspects of the instructional programme, and to define problems they face in teaching. The responses, as might be expected, are confidential. The Teaching Practice Survey contains 32 items on teaching activities in which instructors might engage (e.g. video-taping class sessions for diagnostic purposes) and teaching procedures they might use (e.g. frequency with which lectures, demonstrations, tutorials are used). This survey can be given either individually or in a group setting. Again the results are confidential.

Employing these instruments with an appropriate sample of staff members has proved to be no easy matter. For this reason we have chosen first to determine the 'state of the art' of teaching practice at Illinois State. That is, we have tried to determine what characterises the teaching and attitudes of those who could be described as 'instructional leaders'. By securing information on teaching as practiced by this group, we would have a foundation for further investigations, as well as a bench mark against which to compare new data. This has meant concentrating our efforts on collecting baseline data from staff members who have been recognised in some way as superior teachers and/or have demonstrated their concern for quality instruction. Seventy-five staff members have been identified as leaders in instruction through nominations by administrators and staff, receipt of university grants for instructional innovation, and participation on a voluntary basis in certain Center activities.

In obtaining information about student perceptions of teaching and about problems with teaching practice identified by students, we have used results from the Institutional Student Survey,[4] and the Environmental Assessment Inventory.[5] The Institutional Student Survey is based upon measures prepared by the Higher Education Evaluation Program under the directorship of C. Robert Pace and was last administered to some 4,000 students in 1974. Of particular significance as baseline measures are the sections on ratings of instructional quality, perceptions of courses and faculty, and satisfaction with various instructional formats. The Environmental Assessment Inventory has been developed by personnel in the Student Counselling Center at Illinois State and provides a means to monitor continuously the impact of the campus environment, including one factor termed 'academic format', upon various facets of student life. This assessment is done by staff assistants in the residence halls and has been carried on for about ten months. Because these data are available to us, we have not as yet tried to devise instruments to measure student perceptions of teaching practice which might be more directly related to our staff development work.

Results

The data we have thus far are only tentative and should be treated as such. They reveal that students consider human relations goals (e.g. social and personal development) to be of primary importance; the staff consider human relations goals less important by comparison, and rate critical thinking goals as most important. Effective communications and intellectual honesty receive the highest staff ratings. Students consider they are making the most progress on goals of tolerance and social development and the least on vocational training. The staff, however, view progress in vocational training as significant.

When examining students' response to instruction, we find that 80 per cent rate quality of classes in their major subjects as excellent or good; only about 50 per cent rate their general education classes in the same way. While 69 per cent say instructors give students enough opportunities to ask questions and express points of view and 70 per cent believe instructors clearly explain the goals and purposes of their classes, at the same time, 59 per cent believe that personality, pull, and bluff get students through many classes, and 50 per cent say standards set by professors are not particularly hard to achieve. Less than half think instructors make sufficient distinctions between major and lesser ideas (49 per cent), or that most instructors are concerned with being excellent teachers (48 per cent).

With respect to instructional formats, we find that the most frequently encountered formats are the large lecture class and the small class with discussions led by the instructor. Less than one-third participate in some form of independent study. Three-fourths express satisfaction with the small class, but only about a third express satisfaction with the large lecture. The small class with discussion led by the instructor receives the highest rating of all formats (79 per cent satisfied), though surprisingly only 18 per cent think the discussions are vigorous and intense. Videotaped lectures receive the lowest ratings (22 per cent satisfied). Another format receiving unsatisfactory ratings is the self-instructional package in a learning laboratory setting (33 per cent satisfied). Laboratory formats are rated about neutral at the beginning of a term and ratings become increasingly more negative. The only positively rated time for scheduling classes is in the afternoon (and no more than an hour in length) except, it should be noted, in April. Evaluation procedures (either continuous assessment or term examinations) are universally considered in a negative light! Our students do not like tests.

What has emerged, then, is a picture of student satisfaction which reflects a conventional view of instruction. They seem to prefer the traditional American single-teacher class with fewer than 30 students, conducted in a 'discussion' format, even though they do not find the discussions very stimulating. The students are not favourably inclined toward newer instructional procedures such as television and self-instructional materials.

It should perhaps come as no surprise that the instructional leaders on the staff are quite as conventional as most in their teaching. Procedures used with some degree of regularity by over 90 per cent of this group include textbooks, lectures, instructor-led discussions, supplementary readings, 'homework' exercises, and written papers. Some 86 per cent have never used computer-assisted instruction, 53 per cent have never used television, and 58 per cent have never used self-instructional packages. On the other hand, these are the procedures most frequently indicated by the instructional leaders (though still less than one-third) as ones they would like to try.

This group of instructors indicates that during the last three years more than 90 per cent have personally constructed the examinations they use; these examinations usually contain both 'objective' and 'essay' items. Over 95 per cent regularly use a standardised departmental form for student evaluation of teaching, though they do not do much formal analysis of their own teaching. About two-thirds have never audio-taped class or lecture sessions; three-fourths have not used videotape for this purpose, and 60 per cent have not used any techniques to determine patterns of classroom interaction. But these are the teaching-analysis activities the leaders would like to try.

These instructors would rate at least three-fourths of their departmental colleagues as attaching 'high importance' to teaching and performing at a 'good' or 'superior' level in their teaching. By comparison, some 90 per cent of the staff have been rated in the top two of five teaching performance categories in the university's staff evaluation system.

Even if they perceive teaching to be carried on in a manner that is quite acceptable, the instructional leaders have identified some problem areas. They are particularly concerned with the lack of communication and discussion among themselves about teaching and how to improve the quality of teaching practice. They feel the need for closer working relationships among those who are trying new approaches to instruction. Though these staff members have devoted considerable effort to their teaching, they believe there is a lack of institutional reward for teaching, and they question whether the climate at Illinois State University really is supportive of those who expend the energy necessary for improvement. Class sizes at the undergraduate level are thought by these instructors to be too large for effective teaching as they would like to practice it. In this connection it should be noted that the average size for undergraduate classes is about 28. As might be expected, there is some sentiment that students are not as motivated or capable as they could be.

Conclusions

What interpretation we in a staff development center should make of all this information is not at all clear. If our staff members are as competent as the data from colleagues suggest, then perhaps they do not need to be 'developed' at all. The information from students does not exactly confirm this conclusion, however. We have used the baseline data in setting up workshops on small group discussion procedures and have established a communications network among staff members to disseminate information about developments in teaching. Among other activities we are planning are workshops on lecture organisation and delivery skills.

It could be argued that these are commonsense activities and could be undertaken without reference to any baseline data at all. But the matter is not quite that simple. Students like small classes, even if the discussion is not very stimulating, but do they actually want to be involved in such discussions? Perhaps their satisfaction with such classes will diminish, even as the quality of teaching improves. Should we encourage instructional innovation utilising the latest technology when both students and staff members seem more satisfied with the conventional? Should we train staff to be better at lecturing or attempt to provide them with alternatives in a situation which may not reward change? Should we do both? The answers to these questions are not readily apparent.

Admittedly we still have only an incomplete picture of the status of teaching practice, but we think this can be remedied. We will continue our interviews and include staff members who do not qualify as leaders, who in fact might be termed 'low achievers', as well as those in the middle range. We are in the process of constructing an instrument, using the 'balanced incomplete block' technique, to get better information about the frequency with which students encounter various teaching procedures. We plan to begin interviewing students and to use small group sessions in much the same way we have with faculty. And, most important, we intend to concentrate on constructing more objective measures of teaching proficiency.

When this study is completed, there will at least be a rather comprehensive set of baseline data on the status of teaching practice at one large institution. There will also be available a set of instruments for securing baseline data which can then be tested for generality of application and adapted for use in other staff development programmes. To extend the metaphor from the title of this paper, we have taken some first steps in securing baseline data on teaching practice, rather stumbling steps to be sure, and we are making some progress on our journey into staff development.

Notes and References

1 See: WEGIN, Jon F. et al (1976) The practice of faculty development Journal of Higher Education 47 (3) 289-308

2 HEATH, Robert W. and NIELSON, M.A. (1974) The research basis for performance-based teacher education Review of Educational Research 44 (4) 463-484

3 Institutional Goals Inventory: Summary of Results (1975) Illinois State University Office of Undergraduate Instruction

4 Institutional Student Survey, Report No. 2 (1974) Illinois State University Measurement and Evaluation Service

5 CONYNE, Robert J. (1975) Environmental assessment: mapping for counsellor action Personnel and Guidance Journal 54 (3) 151-154

- (1976) The Impact of the ISU Campus Environment on Students Through Use of the Environmental Assessment Inventory Illinois State University Student Counselling Center

6 JOHNSON, Henry C., RHODES, Dent M. and RUMERY, R.E. (1975) The assessment of teaching in higher education: a critical retrospect and a proposal Higher Education 4 (2) 173-199; 4 (3) 273-404

5. STAFF DEVELOPMENT THROUGH EVALUATION

Helping Doctors Become Better Teachers: by becoming Course Evaluators

Dr. R. Cox (with N. Rea and S. Robinson) (University Teaching Methods Unit)

The Contribution of Student Feedback to Staff Development

P. Ramsden (University of Lancaster)

Staff Development Through Self-Evaluation

Professor L. R. B. Elton (University of Surrey)

HELPING DOCTORS BECOME BETTER TEACHERS: BY BECOMING COURSE EVALUATORS

by Roy Cox, Nicolas Rea and Sarah Robinson, University Teaching Methods Unit, University of London

In 1970 the University Teaching Methods Unit were asked to take part in the British Postgraduate Medical Federation course for teachers in general practice which lasted 24 half-days over nine months. The teachers were all established general practitioners who were or were hoping to become 'trainers' of general practice to newly qualified doctors — usually on an apprenticeship basis. The evaluation project which began in 1971 was at that time seen primarily as a means of developing methods of evaluation to be used by course organisers as a means of improving their courses. After six years' development, however, it became clear that the more significant part of course evaluation was not generating information useful to course organisers but integrating the participants' evaluation into the learning activities in such a way that their experiences became more personally significant to them.[1] With two of the earlier courses evaluation became highly significant when it concerned whether or not they should continue. The first revolt was against over-structuring, the second against under-structuring but in both cases the involvement in rethinking the course and commitment to the new one was impressive. Later courses hearing of this felt there was something lacking in their own courses but benefitted we think from changes in the role of evaluation.

During the project several evaluation methods were developed and these are discussed below.

a) Inventory on Attitudes to Teaching in General Practice

This was used in a number of ways, but it was designed originally to give us an idea of how far attitudes were changing during the course. Participants became involved in evaluation when they compared their individual responses at the end of the course with those at the beginning. Discussions about the changes were interesting to both participants and organisers but we hope to make these more focused and more useful in future by discussing them in terms of the factors. These are concerned with participation, teaching style, commitment, management of learning and interpersonal relationships.

b) The Use of Comments on Tape-recorded Teaching

Participants evaluated short (5-10 minutes) tape-recorded examples of actual teaching. A measure of progress on the course was obtained by asking for comments by course members on the same example of teaching at the beginning and again at the end of the course. (An extract from one of these examples was given at the conference.) Comments on teaching points were written down during a ten-minute period after the tape has finished. Rating them against a 'master list' of comments made on each example by course organisers and course participants made us examine critically the way in which they might reflect the attitudes and knowledge encouraged by the course. The 'before' and 'after' comments were given back to each participant at the end of the course. These formed a basis for informal discussion and reinforcement of points made on the course. Gains in educational awareness were observed in most (not all) participants.

c) Course Diaries

Members kept a weekly diary, in which they commented on the use and interest of the educational, medical and social aspects of each session. The following week the top copy was handed to the researcher and a copy served as a record for the writer. This gave members an opportunity to reflect on the progress and content of the course, and to evaluate its relevance to their work as teachers in general practice.

What contribution can keeping a course diary make to the process of helping doctors to become better teachers? Four main areas have been identified from studying the diaries:

(i) It provides them with a permanent record of the events and contents of the course.

(ii) It gives them the opportunity after the session is over to consider what they have learnt and to relate this to their own experience and development both as doctors and as teachers.

(iii) It gives them the opportunity to evaluate the various teaching methods they have seen in practice on the course, and this has encouraged them to consider how they could use these in helping their trainees to learn about general practice.

(iv) It provides an opportunity to reflect on the dynamics of the course at work, i.e. on the way the various tasks have been tackled, on the inter-relationships between participants, and on the tensions and friendships which have been generated.

Some course members have shown a substantial change in writing style as the course has progressed, moving away from recapitulation, to analyse the content of the course and the relationships between its members, and then increasingly to relate this to their own development. We have been studying the extent to which these changes appear to be correlated with similar changes as revealed by the other measures described.

Data from the diaries has been regularly reported back to the course members, and further discussion and reflection has been generated by learning about other people's perceptions and opinions.

Members' Reports on the Course

The diaries were closely interrelated with two other methods of course evaluation

(i) Individual reports on last week's session presented at the beginning of the afternoon. Some doctors just summarised the content of the session, whilst others focused on the tensions which developed between groups of doctors who had very different ideas concerning the purpose of the course.

(ii) Group mid-course and end of course reports: these also encouraged the course members to reflect on previous sessions, but additionally they provided a forum in which groups of doctors had to work out their common perceptions of events.

e) Post Course Evaluation

Finally there were both post course and long-term interviews and questionnaires which for many provided a useful opportunity to stand back and review their nine months' involvement. It was this constant and often deep reflection upon what was happening to them educationally and personally that is likely to produce lasting changes not only in relation to their teaching but to their work as general practitioners.

Notes and References

1 Despite the growing emphasis on less formal evaluation there has been little written about this. Even PARLETT, M. and HAMILTON, D. (1972) in their influential Evaluation as Illumination: a new approach to the study of innovatory programmes, mimeo University of Edinburgh, do not discuss the educational role of student involvement in evaluation.
GOLDSCHMID, B. and GOLDSCHMID, M. (1975) in Peer Teaching in Higher Education: a review, Lausanne, Ecole Polytechnique Federale, discuss student participation thoroughly but have little to say about evaluation. The idea has been developed by HERON, J. (1974) The Concept of a Peer Learning Community, University of Surrey, Centre for Adult Education, and is discussed in COX, R. (1974) Formative Evaluation: interpretation and participation in CROMBAG, H. and DE GRUYTER, D. (eds.) Contemporary Issues in Education Testing The Hague, Mouton

THE CONTRIBUTION OF STUDENT FEEDBACK TO STAFF DEVELOPMENT

by Paul Ramsden, Institute for Research and Development in Post-Compulsory Education, University of Lancaster

I wish to do three things in this paper. I shall outline a questionnaire system of student evaluation of teaching which has been in use at North East London Polytechnic (NELP) during the last two years.[1] I will then consider four potential areas of usefulness of this method to academic staff development, and draw upon lecturers' comments on the NELP procedures to illustrate my arguments. Finally, I shall examine the limitations and problems of this type of student feedback applied to staff development and consider the implications of these difficulties for future activities in this field.

The Questionnaire

Over 100 NELP staff from nearly every department of the Polytechnic have used a standard feedback questionnaire designed at NELP which consists of a number of statements describing teaching behaviours and attitudes. A teacher using this voluntary system arranges for questionnaires to be given out to his students. The completed forms can be returned to a central unit for analysis; alternatively the teacher works out the scores for himself. Questionnaires sent to the central unit are dealt with in strict confidence. The questionnaires comprise two sections: in the first, students rate — on a five-point scale for each question — the performance of the lecturer. In the second section, students rate the relative importance of each of the items. The results returned to teachers provide a straightforward summary of the mean values of each item in both sections, and also show the list of items in rank order of mean value. This makes it possible to identify at a glance students' perceptions of the teaching strengths and weaknesses of a lecturer, and to note the relative importance attached by the student group to each statement. At an early stage, the NELP project rejected the possibility of using student evaluations as an indicator of a teacher's performance compared to that of other teachers, so that (for example), decisions about promotion and tenure might be made from the results. There is a growing body of evidence against this usage.[2] I do not propose to rehearse the arguments again here, but it is worth remarking that it is regrettable that so much effort has been expended, and continues to be expended — especially in America — in trying to make rating scales and techniques of analysis more sophisticated, in the hope that this will make student evaluations valid as comparisons of teachers' performance. Improved techniques cannot make ill-founded principles right. A greater concentration on relatively simple diagnostic procedures might well have been more fruitful. It is the problems and possibilities of this sort of scheme which I consider below.

Use in Staff Development

The first potential contribution of student feedback is to help staff to identify for themselves student-perceived teaching strengths and weaknesses; to help them gain information on how closely their students' expectations of them match their students' ratings; and to help staff to make changes to their teaching which will improve it. Teachers using the NELP system have been asked to comment on its effectiveness; all users are either interviewed or asked to provide written comments on the use they make of the results. Many participants have been able to diagnose problems and to deal with them because of using the questionnaire. Staff have either had their suspicions about their teaching weaknesses confirmed from the questionnaire results or have discovered that their own perceptions of students' views were incorrect. A teacher who was rated low by his students for his organisation of subject matter took steps to state teaching objectives more clearly before each class session. One teacher who thought himself to be easily accessible for private discussion of students' work found that his students thought him difficult to contact. Another lecturer realised that his writing on the blackboard was illegible to students.

The second contribution of student feedback is to help lecturers increase their awareness of the problems of teaching and learning and to encourage them to think more actively about their teaching aims and objectives. Many NELP staff have pointed to these advantages. There were several remarks to the effect that using the questionnaire had made staff think more deeply about what they were doing as teachers and about how their teaching related to students' learning. A number of staff mentioned the fact that knowledge of students' expectations of them as teachers, gained from section 2 of the questionnaire, had proved very valuable. Some teachers have been able to gain information on different students' reactions to them and to adapt their teaching accordingly. One lecturer noted the much greater difficulty overseas students had in following his presentation. Another found that evening class students rated the importance of his ability to encourage student discussion less highly than full-time students; after consultation with both groups, he adapted his teaching strategies accordingly.

The third use of student feedback is to help create a more relaxed and understanding relationship between a teacher and his students, so that students become more willing to offer constructive criticism. It may seem odd that a formal questionnaire on a lecturer's classroom performance should be the beginning of a more accepting relationship between teacher and students, but many NELP staff mentioned this contribution. Lecturers cited cases in which classes discussed the questionnaire results with them and raised points not covered in the questionnaire or expanded on the results. Several staff remarked that asking students to assess oneself was an expression of confidence in their judgement. Thus better and closer relationships became possible afterwards. 'I worry a lot about my teaching' (said one lecturer) 'and the exercise helped me to appreciate how it is going. It also helped to create a stronger link between myself and the students. They appreciated the chance to help, I think.'

The fourth potential contribution of feedback questionnaires is to provide information on aspects of dissatisfaction with teaching within the whole of a college or university, so that implications for staff development needs and training programmes can be drawn out. By comparing the differences between the rank orders assigned by students to the first section of the NELP questionnaire (student ratings of individual teachers) and the second section (student ratings of the importance of each item), for all teachers who have used the system and returned results, we can obtain a fairly crude measure of relative dissatisfaction. The areas of greatest dissatisfaction for NELP students in this study were: clarity of lecturers' explanations; lecturers' ability to stimulate students to think independently; presentation of material in a well-organised way; constructiveness of lecturers' comments on written work.

Problems and Limitations

What are the problems and limitations of the techniques used at NELP? It is doubtful, firstly, whether the information is appropriate for offering general guidelines for staff development needs in the Polytechnic, for the following reasons. The staff using the method are unlikely to be representative of all staff; although there is no evidence to support the assertion that they are teachers who are most confident about their performance in the classroom, this seems intuitively likely. On more than one occasion, for example, students have commented that the lecturers who would benefit from improving their teaching techniques are among those who do not use feedback questionnaires. Other reasons for doubting the usefulness of evaluation results for providing information about staff development needs in the whole institution include the fact that individual teachers' profiles of strengths and weaknesses shown in the results vary considerably from one teacher to another; that the items in the questionnaire are a limited selection of teaching skills; and that students' judgements may be biased in ways which we cannot control.

Several of the difficulties experienced in the NELP study illustrate the characteristic tension in staff development activities between institutional requirements (or teachers' perceptions of institutional requirements) and individual needs. There were problems connected with confidentiality, the threat posed by asking for student evaluations, in encouraging the use of the system, with the design of the questionnaire, and with helping staff to make constructive use of the results. Some teachers found the questionnaire inappropriate to their teaching methods, and there is no doubt that a standardised form is likely to be too rigid to be applicable to all teaching situations and to every course. The questionnaire used emphasises lecturing techniques at the expense of skills in small group and individual teaching.[3] It ignores the fact that some teachers have special requirements, such as questions relevant to part-time students.

Other difficulties were experienced in the study in encouraging staff to use the questionnaires and to continue to use them regularly. Some teachers doubted the confidentiality of the results and were worried that the system might be used for institutional monitoring of individual lecturers' teaching. 'Yes' (a colleague might say) 'your evaluation system is <u>now</u> voluntary, confidential, and concerned with feedback rather than assessment. But if I co-operate now, who is to say whether in two or three years' time the system will be the same? If a majority of teachers used the system, would this not be an argument for management to institute compulsory monitoring?' Quite apart from the question of confidentiality, student evaluation poses a threat to a lecturer; and it is probable that it poses a very great threat to those lecturers, paradoxically, who need to improve their teaching most.[4]

Perhaps the most serious limitation of the NELP inquiry has been the lack of a co-ordinated relationship between student feedback methods and procedures to enable staff to deal with teaching difficulties. Encouragement and help to act upon the questionnaire results, and to remedy teaching weaknesses which are seen to be real ones by a lecturer and by his students, has been missing. The problem is to devise schemes which do not compromise the individual responsibility and confidentiality of diagnostic feedback.

Several of the difficulties considered above will, it is hoped, be met by changes to the procedures currently in use at NELP. The emphasis will continue to be on a service to staff which is deliberately related to their self-defined needs. In order to overcome the problem of a questionnaire which is seen to be inappropriate to some sorts of teaching situations, individual members of staff are now able to construct their own questionnaires from a bank of items, and other standardised questionnaires are being developed. Methods other than questionnaires, especially group discussions with students, are also being tested. The scope of the original project will be widened to include other forms of evaluation, including co-operative exercises in the observation of teaching by colleagues. Staff who have used feedback methods will be encouraged much more strongly to discuss the results with project members, and to share them with colleagues and students. Programmes of seminars will be arranged at which users of the system can consider the introduction of changes to teaching strategies based on the results of evaluations.

Conclusions

In spite of these changes, there are aspects of student evaluation which are likely to remain problematic, and it is worthwhile to summarise them. They are:

a) In a voluntary system, most staff will probably not wish to participate.

b) The exercise of having one's teaching performance assessed by students is, and is likely to continue to be, a very threatening exercise for most teachers; especially for those who are least confident. Student evaluation may not be the best way of helping this group.

c) Although every assurance is given, staff will be suspicious of the privacy of a confidential system of evaluation. Once again, the teachers who are least sure of themselves may well be the most doubtful.

d) The most intractable problem is that of much educational research: what happens to the results. It will often prove difficult to persuade teachers to act on the results, even though they accept them as valid.

None of these problems, however, should be taken as arguments against the use of student feedback techniques. But it is always well to know the limitations of one's methods. Student feedback places a heavy responsibility upon teachers themselves to use it and to act on its findings; here lie both its main strengths and principal drawbacks. The NELP study has demonstrated the usefulness of questionnaire methods of student evaluation in three fields :

a) As a means of enabling lecturers to find out for themselves their students' opinions of their teaching, in a way which ensures that every student has an opportunity to comment anonymously.

b) As a means of stimulating staff to think more about their teaching aims.

c) As a way of helping to build better relationships between lecturers and students.

These benefits suggest that diagnostic methods of teacher evaluation could be used much more extensively than they are at present in Britain as an effective means of staff development.

The introduction of these methods will have to be sensitively carried out, most especially in a climate of restricted resources and low growth in higher education. It has been said that improvement in teaching in higher education can only take place to the extent that we give teachers the opportunity to reflect more closely on what they do, how they are doing it, and how their students react to what they do. Student feedback methods which are responsive to staff needs and quite separate from institutional procedures for assessing staff performance offer one way of helping lecturers to improve their teaching; and we may hope, thereby, to improve the experience of learning for their students.

Notes and References

1 The research on which this paper is based was carried out at NELP in collaboration with Philip S. Bradbury while the author was Research Fellow in the college's Student Feedback Project, 1973-1976.

2 See, for example:

FLOOD PAGE, C. (1974) Student Evaluation of Teaching: the American experience London, SRHE

JOHNSON, H.C., RHODES, D.M. and RUMERY, R.E. (1975) The assessment of teaching in higher education: a critical retrospect and a proposal Part I: A critical retrospect Higher Education 4 173-199

RAMSDEN, P. (1975) Polytechnic students' expectations of their teachers and the use of a student feedback questionnaire: a preliminary report Higher Education Bulletin 3 (2) 73-85

3 There are difficulties in using closed-ended questionnaires to evaluate teaching with small groups of students. Chief among these is the problem of unreliability of results from groups of less than twenty-five. One solution is to combine the results of several smaller groups.

4 Another group of staff who are unlikely to use feedback methods are those who are simply not conscious of any need to improve their teaching, although their students may see great need.

STAFF DEVELOPMENT THROUGH SELF-EVALUATION

by L.R.B. Elton, Institute for Educational Technology, University of Surrey

Introduction

One of the best kept secrets in university teaching is the evidence that academics do not necessarily improve through practice. Best kept and secret because teaching has been so essentially private an activity in universities,[1] and yet we all know of academic staff well into middle age who are still inaudible, still unable to complete their lectures on time, still embarrassed when teaching small groups, still unaware of their aims or that they are not achieving them. As Thorndike demonstrated many years ago,[2] practice without knowledge of results does not lead to learning, and the almost complete lack of feedback that is a feature of much university teaching is the likely cause of the phenomenon mentioned above.

One comparatively painless way to obtain such feedback is through means that allow one to evaluate one's own work without involving one's colleagues. I wish now to discuss some of these.

Some Methods of Self-evaluation

The most widely used method is the student questionnaire for the evaluation of lectures. As this has been the subject of the previous talk, I just want to mention one development of it in which two of my research students, Vivien Hodgson and David McConnell, are engaged. They have used the Kelly repertory grid with undergraduate students in order to generate the questions on the questionnaire in terms of student perception, and they have in this way also been able to produce questionnaires that deal with particular aspects of teacher performance. These questionnaires are at present undergoing first trials.

Next, Will Bridge has constructed a quite comprehensive set of materials,[3] called Monitor kit, which enables a member of staff to evaluate a course that is based on individual learning, such as the Keller plan, and another student of mine, Mario Lopez, is at present engaged in producing a similar kit for the evaluation of resource centres.

A colleague of mine, Sid O'Connell, has been lending academics a complete TV camera chain and monitor to take home in the boot of their car, so that they could put in some practice and observe themselves without being observed. We should all use at least an audio-tape recorder and perhaps a mirror, in the way actors do, to practise our conference presentations.

A practice that is common in the Civil Service and the Armed Forces is to have to fill in annually a form on which one gives an account of what one has done in the past year. Such forms exist in some American Universities, e.g. the University of Massachusetts,[4] and could be most valuable here. For probationers, this practice could be linked to the fulfilment of a contract that had been negotiated at the beginning of the year.

Assessment of Teaching

This brings me to the vexed question as to how to assess academics, and in particular probationers, on their performance as teachers.[1] I am convinced that we should experiment with methods by which teachers evaluate themselves and then make the results of such an evaluation available for scrutiny.

Conclusion

I have mentioned some methods of self-evaluation that are already available, others that are still at the development stage and some that have not got beyond the realm of ideas. What is important is to make a start soon and to make it with the young. For as Paul Valery has said: 'Long years must pass before the truths we have made for ourselves become our very flesh.'

Notes and References

1 ELTON, L.R.B. (1975) Is it possible to assess teaching? Evaluating Teaching in Higher Education London, UTMU

2 Quoted by W.J. McKeachie in ENTWISTLE, N. and HOUNSELL, D. (eds.) (1975) How Students Learn Lancaster, University of Lancaster, p.43

3 BRIDGE, W.A. (1976) Monitor kit obtainable from Institute for Educational Technology, University of Surrey

4 WOODBURY, R.L. (1975) The politics of teacher evaluation and improvement: a look at the United States Evaluating Teaching in Higher Education London, UTMU

6. INSTITUTIONALIZATION

The Nature of the Controls Surrounding Academic Activity

Dr. R. Startup (University College, Swansea)

The Contribution of Educational Development Services to Staff Development in Polytechnics

Dr. S. Trickey (Sheffield City Polytechnic)

Staff Development Leave: Policy and Practice

Miss H. K. Greenaway (Polytechnic of North London) with Dr. A. Harding (University of Bradford)

THE NATURE OF THE CONTROLS SURROUNDING ACADEMIC ACTIVITY

by Richard Startup, M. A., Ph. D., Department of Sociology and Anthropology, University College, Swansea

For some years I have been engaged in a sociological study of the role of the university teacher. This has included a detailed analysis of the various activities of staff within a particular provincial university. In this paper I will focus on a particular aspect of the wider investigation, namely the system of control which operates within the university to regulate academic activity. This is a fundamental element of a role study because it has to do with the incentives and rewards which account for observable patterns in the behaviour of university teachers.

I judge that the topic of this paper links intimately to the theme of the conference. It is only fruitful to examine issues of staff training and development jointly with a consideration of the control mechanisms which function within the university. Systems of sanctions — for example salary scales and promotion procedures — serve to encourage certain kinds of development and they inhibit others. This carries implications for reform within the university.

In this study there were two main periods of data collection. A survey of all the staff at a particular provincial university was conducted and 190 university teachers completed questionnaires, giving a 52 per cent response rate. It can be shown that the obtained sample of staff was reasonably representative along certain important dimensions for which information is available from university records. (E. g. when the distribution of the sample of staff between the two sexes, the five faculties and the four grades is compared with that in the population, in no case is the difference greater than that which results from random fluctuations).

The second phase of data collection consisted of interviews with staff. A department was selected from each of the four faculties of the university (excluding Education) and every staff member was interviewed The chosen departments — classics, pure mathematics, civil engineering and psychology — were in certain respects typical of departments in their respective faculties. In addition, four other departmental heads were selected and interviewed.

Intrinsic Rewards

Initially we must examine how intrinsically rewarding staff found various parts of their job to be. This is an important area to consider in an analysis of control mechanisms. For one thing, intrinsic rewards serve to channel activity (both in more and less approved directions). In addition, an understanding of intrinsic rewards is needed so that the operation and effectiveness of systems of sanctions can be evaluated. We need to know, for instance, what sanctions existed to encourage the performance of relatively unrewarding but important activities.

When (during the interviews) the staff members were asked how intrinsically rewarding they found the various aspects of their job, they sometimes commented on specific detailed aspects, e.g. lecturing, tutorial work and marking (this latter was particularly unpopular). However, though they varied in the extent to which they went into detail, most staff were able to specify how relatively rewarding they found their three main activities — teaching, research and administration. They were able to say which they found (a) most rewarding, (b) second most rewarding, and (c) least rewarding.

Generally speaking, where the staff member was able to choose a most rewarding activity, it proved to be either teaching or research and, in fact, rather more respondents selected research (41 per cent) than teaching (25 per cent). However, as many as 30 per cent found teaching and research to be equally rewarding. Only two respondents out of 44 stated that administration was the most rewarding of the three kinds of activity.

Research emerged as generally the most rewarding activity, partly because of the distinctive pattern of responses in a single department: Classics. Five out of six classicists selected research as most rewarding, while the staff of the three other departments tended to divide up fairly equally between those favouring research and those favouring teaching. Interestingly, in the Classics Department in the recent past there had been many innovations in teaching. Staff teaching 'loads' were considered to be heavy (particularly those of junior staff) and the departmental head stated that within his department teaching effectively carried more weight than research. Given the disparity between the priority of the department and individual staff preferences, it is not surprising that considerable unease was generated. In none of the other three departments was there this type of problem.

Bearing these patterns in mind we next examine some other influences on staff activity.

The Control Exercised by the Departmental Head

At departmental level the central controlling figure was the professorial departmental head. Everyone saw the head as being responsible for inter alia the organisation of teaching, the maintenance of teaching standards, the channelling of research into the department (particularly in the applied sciences) and the administrative working of the department. The head was required to make sure that these various tasks were appropriately performed and it was the duty of other staff to assist him as effectively as they could.

Since the head was required to exercise a control function, his colleagues expected him to react positively or negatively towards their activities and achievements. Some heads (but not all) attached considerable importance to this part of their role. One said that 'you must encourage people to be successful'. Another allied way in which the head exercised a constraining influence was through his control over departmental resources. Among other things this enabled him to confer or withold patronage; he could, for instance, offer better facilities to senior staff. Indeed this was a conventional practice.

But the chief way in which the head could influence the conduct of his staff was through his control over the progress of their careers — more especially at the key points of gaining (or failing to gain) tenure, passing (or failing to pass) through the efficiency bar and earning or failing to earn promotion to the grade of senior lecturer or reader. At these various stages, though the key decision was taken by a university committee, information of crucial importance was sought from the departmental head. In the case of promotion the head's influence was even greater for it was normal for him to take the initiative in putting forward the names of candidates from among his staff. An awareness of these various procedures affected the staff evaluation of the departmental head. Nor did his influence end there, for a lecturer applying for a job elsewhere was expected to give the name of his departmental head as a reference.

Yet if departmental heads had considerable powers did they exercise their control function effectively? Apparently not always and the case of teaching is illustrative. In two of the four selected departments it was extremely rare for the head himself to initiate any discussion of possible teaching problems with new staff members. Another piece of evidence is that the heads' self-assessed knowledge of their colleagues' qualities as teachers was highly variable. Three of the eight heads interviewed felt that they had rather limited knowledge of their colleagues' qualities as teachers. One reason for lack of knowledge was that (by convention) heads did not normally attend their colleagues' formal teaching sessions. Where relevant knowledge was lacking the head was simply not in a position actively to maintain teaching standards, although he was expected to do so by a majority of staff. This is particularly significant in view of the finding reported above, that rather fewer staff selected teaching than research as the activity which they found most intrinsically rewarding. There could be no justification for assuming that all staff would automatically devote an appropriate amount of their time and energy to teaching. (For a more extended analysis of the head's role, see Startup (1976))

Salaries

Having examined control within the department, consideration must next be paid to the system of financial rewards which operated on a university-wide basis. That system possessed two main elements. The first was the way in which those in the career grade — the lecturer grade — were paid. The principle which had come into general use was the 'wage for age' principle viz. that lecturers of the same age should receive the same salary. This system involves all lecturers being paid on a single incremental scale with a fixed starting point at age 26. The second main element in the reward system was the procedure for promotion into higher grades.

When they were interviewed the staff members were first asked whether they felt that the 'wage for age' principle was the appropriate way in which to determine how much lecturers should be paid. Altogether 68 per cent felt that it was indeed the best dominant principle, though many staff felt that there should be scope for minor modifications in individual cases. The remaining 32 per cent of staff denied the appropriateness of the 'wage for age' principle itself. Among these latter the most widespread worry concerned the lack of effectiveness of this principle as an incentive. Another basis upon which some staff challenged the principle was by reference to the need for a flexible system, so that the university could bargain to make the most suitable appointments.

There were also comments and objections which were more frequently forthcoming from those teaching particular subjects. It seems that the perceived effectiveness and appropriateness of the age related scale varied in an interesting way depending upon discipline.

Among the civil engineers there was least support for the 'wage for age' principle. Only half the staff favoured it. Some wanted academic salaries to match the emoluments obtainable by the professional engineer in the outside world.

Among the pure mathematicians, too, some doubts were expressed about the effectiveness of the 'wage for age' principle, though as many as two thirds of the staff seemed to be on balance in favour of it. The problem here centred on the perceived anomaly whereby a young mathematician earned less than an older colleague, even if he were more brilliant and more productive in a research sense. It was in fact among the psychologists and classicists where there was most support for the 'wage for age' principle. Eighty per cent of these staff favoured it. It seems that neither of these two disciplines experienced to any marked degree the problem of unusual precosity (which arose in pure mathematics) nor the problem of staff being drawn away from the university by higher financial rewards obtainable elsewhere (which arose in engineering).

Despite an awareness of certain anomalies, there was no widely supported alternative to the 'wage for age' principle. On this evidence, it seems unlikely that there will be a sustained move among staff to challenge the existing system. Yet it may be judged that in connection with the lecturers' salary scale there is no close connection between effort or achievement and financial reward. The situation was one where a premium appeared to be placed on the dedication of the academic to his job. It also meant that promotion procedures were critically important, for the prospect of promotion constituted a major incentive to do more than 'the minimum'.

The Staff View of Promotion Procedures

In the university, appointments to the senior lecturer and reader grades almost invariably took the form of internal promotions. As indicated above, the names of candidates for promotion were generally submitted to the appropriate university committee by departmental heads. The formal criteria linked promotion to a readership with exceptional performance in research, while the senior lectureship was associated with all-round performance. These were the formal criteria, but how did staff see the operation of the process?

When asked (in the survey) to indicate how satisfied they were with the promotion procedures, only 14 per cent of staff said that they were satisfied, while as many as 45 per cent expressed varying degrees of dissatisfaction and over one third had mixed (balanced) reactions. Even among those already promoted there were more dissatisfied (18) than satisfied (14) with the prevailing system and a further 24 had mixed (balanced) reactions to it. Thus dissatisfaction with promotion procedures was widespread. (For more details of the survey results see Gruneberg _et al_. (1974) and Startup (1975))

In the interviews with staff also, substantial dissatisfaction was expressed with the existing system. It was felt that research effectively carried too much weight in connection with promotion and teaching too little (cf. Halsey and Trow, (1971) p. 349). The view was also frequently put forward that publications were decisive and these counted most in a quantitative rather than in a qualitative sense. Yet, despite the widespread feeling among the staff interviewed that teaching should carry more weight than it in fact did, only a minority favoured the use of a systematic appraisal of student reactions to, or assessments of, teaching. There was the persistent feeling among staff that students were not adequate judges of teaching. We must ourselves indicate though that students were effectively the only 'consumers' of teaching.

Another area considered in the interviews was the question of the mobility of academics between universities and the connection (if any) between mobility and internal promotion systems. Certainly a majority of staff (80 per cent) felt that lecturers were too immobile. A minority advocated making senior appointments open and this, it was felt, would be beneficial to the standards both of teaching and of research, but it was stressed that other universities should do the same. Yet despite their consciousness of the problem of immobility a majority of staff (60 per cent) took a different line: these academics felt that those who had served the university well over an extended period of time had the first claim on promoted positions.

The Regulation of Activity Outside the University

In our examination of control mechanisms, we need finally to consider the regulation of activity initiated from outside the university. There are a number of such activities but in the interests of brevity we shall confine ourselves to a particularly important one: fee paid consultancy work. This type of employment, in which work was initiated by an outside client, had a substantial place in the working lives of the civil engineers, but it was of (at most) peripheral significance for academics in the three other selected departments. The essential difference between civil engineering and the other three disciplines is that the former is *necessarily* applied. The engineers felt it to be their duty to 'keep in touch with the real world'.

It was sometimes stated that a sharp line could not be drawn between consultancy work and research. In order to throw more light on this matter, during the interviews those staff active in consultancy work were asked to say how much of it could be said to have a research content. Their answers varied from 95 per cent to 40 per cent. Therefore it does seem that staff were *sometimes* involved in the solution of routine problems which they saw as lacking a research element. There were also cases where staff had not pursued a research possibility to the point where they published an article, since they had continued with other consultancy work. Thus, one is bound to conclude that consultancy work not only served to generate research, but it also sometimes drew energies away from research and publication.

Those active in consultancy work believed that it generated hostility from elsewhere within the university. The perceived hostility was seen as being linked to the issue of remuneration. Some other staff in the university felt that university based consultants were receiving additional payment for doing something (research) which was part of their job anyway. There was also the point that the research 'problem' on which the consultant worked was decided by his client. There could be seen to be tension between this practice and the traditional conception that the university teacher had security of tenure and reasonable emoluments, so that he could be free to devote himself to whatever lines of inquiry *he* judged to be important. Yet there was no doubt that consultancy work did bring applied scientists into contact with practical problems of a sophisticated kind. This was valued by them quite apart from the financial aspect.

Conclusion

Within the university, sanctions were applied at two main levels — within the individual department and also on a university-wide basis. As the system actually operated, however, these levels were by no means totally distinct. For instance, we have observed that the departmental head had his power over his immediate colleagues enhanced by the fact that he had an important part to play in connection with the university's sanctioning procedures.

The detailed operation of the control mechanisms possessed certain additional singularities and consequences. We must note particularly, that, for (marginally) the largest proportion of staff, research emerged as the most intrinsically rewarding of their main activites. It was also the case that staff generally felt that in connection with the university's reward system research carried most weight. Hence it may be judged that in a number of important respects the reward system which encompassed the university teacher's role was (paradoxically) biased in favour of research and against teaching. As regards the maintenance of teaching standards, the outstanding feature of the existing system of control was that the person in authority (the departmental head) did not directly observe his colleagues' teaching, while the 'consumers' of teaching (the students) were unable to influence the operation of the reward system itself. Taking everything into account it seems that there were insufficient incentives for staff to raise standards and innovate in the teaching sphere.

Another problem area concerns the extent of geographical mobility among staff. We know that in these times of financial stringency there are difficulties enough in this respect. Yet the problem is being compounded by the existence of predominantly internal promotion systems. On the evidence presented here the operation of such a system and the staff viewpoint on it are such that geographical mobility is being effectively discouraged. This must have substantial (probably negative) implications for staff development.

In relation to fee-paid consultancy work it is important not to over simplify. The interconnection between the definition of the academic role and this type of work is complex. One key point is that there are existing systems of control within the university regulating the activity 'research'. Inevitably consultancy work provides a framework of inducements and sanctions which supplements and, to a certain extent, cuts across that pre-existing framework. Yet the engineers — the staff most active in consultancy work — were charged with the responsibility to 'apply' their ideas and tackle 'real problems'. They were therefore subjected to sanctions which drove them towards consultancy work. But it cannot be denied that this created tensions within the university. Arguably consultancy work sometimes drew staff time and energy away from genuinely original research and it may be that the achievement of traditional university objectives will be undermined uless the activity is more tightly regulated.

References

1 GRUNEBERG, M. M., STARTUP, R. and TAPSFIELD, P. (1974) A study of university teachers' satisfaction with promotion procedures <u>The Vocational Aspect of Education</u> XXVI, 64 (Summer) pp. 53-57

2 HALSEY, A. H. and TROW, M. A. (1971) <u>The British Academics</u>, London Faber and Faber

3 STARTUP, R. (1972) How students see the role of university lecturer <u>Sociology</u> 6 (2) (May) pp. 237-254

- (1975) Report on a study of staff perceptions of promotion procedures and the role of the university teacher in _Evaluating Teaching in Higher Education_ London, UTMU pp. 85-93

- (1976) The role of the departmental head _Studies in Higher Education_ 1 (2) pp. 233-243

THE CONTRIBUTION OF EDUCATIONAL DEVELOPMENT SERVICES TO STAFF DEVELOPMENT IN POLYTECHNICS

by Stuart Trickey, Department of Education Services, Sheffield City Polytechnic

In his pamphlet, Training of Polytechnic Teachers, Harding[1] (1974) put into print for the first time information on the structure of units or services in the area of 'educational development' and on the provision of academic staff training schemes as obtained from a survey of 29 polytechnics during the sessions 1972-73 and 1973-74.

This paper briefly analyses a more up to date view of the structure and function of such services or units from a survey[2] carried out at the instigation of the Committee of the Standing Conference on Educational Development Services in Polytechnics (SCEDSIP) in January 1976. This survey gained information from 24 polytechnics on the terms of reference of units or services in this area (including educational technology units); names, grades and functions of staff; accommodation and equipment; and services and courses provided.

The survey showed that almost all the polytechnics have a central unit or units which provide services in the area of educational technology and most have a staff development function too by offering in-service courses for new and experienced staff. Typically, courses provide an introduction to the polytechnic and to teaching methods and assessment, although some on offer deal with issues outside pedagogic areas such as interviewing, academic management, conduct of meetings etc. It is generally only in the last five years that units have taken on their present role and it is only in this time also that most courses for staff have got under way.

In several polytechnics the staff development function is somewhat separate from the educational technology and media services. For example, Manchester Polytechnic has a newly formed Staff Development and Educational Methods Unit in co-existence with a (media) Educational Services Unit. The position at the polytechnics at Brighton, Hatfield, Kingston, South Bank and Trent is similar. It is interesting to note that in some universities such as Sussex[3] and Bradford the two functions are also somewhat separate.

The policy, however, of centralization is not universally accepted. Thames Polytechnic is rethinking its central service policy and Middlesex Polytechnic with 15 teaching sites has no central unit but provides instead a basic media service on most of its major sites.

Comparing Harding's findings with the present survey it is clear that there have been several significant changes in the structure and work of the units in the last two years. One development has been the creation of new units such as at Leicester Polytechnic (Educational Technology Centre) and at Sheffield (Education Services Department). In the latter case, a merger with two colleges of education has made possible the combination of various AV and TV units, resources centres and staff training functions into a single viable department. Institutional mergers have had a profound effect in other polytechnics as well since into the new polytechnics have sometimes come well-established educational technology units from former colleges of education; examples are Sunderland Polytechnic and the Polytechnic of Wales.

Another development has been the strenthening of existing units such as the ones at Oxford and at Plymouth. Across the units as a whole strengthening is apparent from the growth in the range of services provided and improvement in staffing. Generally, numbers of staff have increased and grading levels raised. Five units now have Burnham Department status, four with Grade V heads and one with a Grade III head, all in post. In 1973 only one unit had a Grade V head in post.

Courses for staff have developed too. Mortimer (1975)[4] has shown that between 1972-73 and 1974-75 there was about 50 per cent growth in the number of polytechnics which provided in-house courses for teaching staff. Furthermore, there was a tendency to lengthen in-house courses; seven now have a duration of between 72 and 108 hours (two in 1972-73) and six extend over 108 hours (five in 1972-73). Also, in as many as 12 polytechnics attendance on in-service courses for new staff without teaching experience is mandatory; sometimes clauses are inserted into conditions of service to that effect. In 1972-73 only two polytechnics had that requirement.

An increasingly important feature of the work of educational units is the provision of courses for experienced staff. Such courses include lecturing, academic management, conduct of meetings, microteaching and interaction analysis, assessment, use of AV resources and reprography. SCEDSIP is promoting the development of teaching/learning packages or simulations 'Polypacs or Trypacs' for use with polytechnic staff. An example is SEXABOARD, an examination board simulation exercise, demonstrated at this Conference, which is part of an assessment package.

We cannot expect further changes in the work of the units as institutions reorganise and settle down from the traumas of institutional mergers. The changes will be dramatic if the proposals[5] of the Advisory Committee for the Supply and Training of Teachers (ACSTT) Sub-Committee are accepted, since this will mean compulsory training of all new full-time polytechnic staff who do not have the equivalent of three years' full-time teaching experience or a recognised teacher training qualification.

Notes and References

1 HARDING, A. G. (1974) Training of Polytechnic Teachers London, SRHE

2 TRICKEY, S. (compiler) (1976) Register of Educational Development Services in Polytechnics Standing Conference on Educational Development Services in Polytechnics PETRAS Newcastle upon Tyne Polytechnic

3 MILLER, G. W. (1976) Staff Development Programmes in British Universities and Polytechnics Paris UNESCO pp. 56-60

4 MORTIMER, D. J. (1975) Marked growth in induction courses SCEDSIP Bulletin 5

5 The ACSTT (FE) Report is not yet released by the DES but a summary of its recommendations may be found in NATFHE Journal 5 (1976)

STAFF DEVELOPMENT LEAVE: POLICY AND PRACTICE

by Harriet Greenaway, The Polytechnic of North London, and Alan G. Harding, University of Bradford

In the early 1970s the term 'staff development' appeared in the language of higher education as a synonym for 'training courses in teaching methods'. Since then there has been growing recognition that the practice of teaching could not be considered in isolation from institutional value and reward systems. Staff development has, in consequence, become discussed in more comprehensive terms. The present study seeks to elicit the extent to which institutions have responded by relating institutional perceptions and practices to policies which are implied, approved, or under discussion. 61 university institutions and 31 polytechnics were surveyed by postal questionnaire sent to registrars in June 1976. The meaning of staff development and policies and procedures concerning staff development leave (our term for sabbatical and study leave) were two of the topics examined.

Institutions vary widely in their interpretation of the term 'staff development', from 'the teaching and learning course' to 'all aspects of work in teaching research and administration'. A third of responding institutions viewed staff development as limited to initial courses and seminars for probationers. Half the polytechnics and a slightly lower proportion of universities saw it as extending beyond a training in teaching methods for new staff to a broader view involving all experience within the institution and, more specifically, institutional support for the professional growth of all academic staff. This broad interpretation exists despite disclaimers, mainly from universities, regarding their lack of use of the term.

If staff development relies on institutional support, institutions might be expected to have some means of ensuring that policies are formulated which can then be recognised and implemented by individuals. That means is normally based on committees of Senate or Academic Board. Their nature and scope vary enormously; so does their ability to produce sound comprehensive policies. In universities committees dealing with staff development leave tend to have procedures rather than explicit policies, and those procedures are couched in terms of establishment resource considerations. This contrasts with the polytechnics' tendency to see the effect of leave in the light of the enhancement of applicant's academic competence.

It is a feature peculiar to higher education that a person is considered to be contributing to the academic community even while he is temporarily removed from his day-to-day involvement in his own institution. The individual benefits, but so do his subject and the institution later. Sabbatical or study leave is an integral part of staff development irrespective of the nature of the academic activity undertaken – hence our preference for the designation 'staff development leave'.

The administrative arrangements for consideration of applications for leave in each institution are understandably different. More important is the question of availability of and implied purpose for leave. Most institutions require an academic to have served a minimum period (two to seven years) before exercising a right to apply. (Fig. 1, p. 94) Very few award sabbatical leave as a right. The most usual length of leave is one term although a third of all responding institutions allow up to one year. As a ratio to qualifying service, leave allowed in polytechnics is more generous than in universities. (Fig. 2, p.95) This appears to be based upon institutional perceptions of the purpose of leave. In universities, leave is more usually given for undisturbed concentration on existing research or scholarship than for study for a further qualification. Most polytechnics, on the other hand, direct their regulations more towards supporting attendance at courses.

There are three possible explanations for this difference. The first relates to the overall ethos of institutions with universities allegedly emphasising research and polytechnics, by ministerial decree, 'primarily teaching institutions'. If this simple, but highly debatable, distinction does underly some of the thinking it is possible that the CNAA's emphasis on the link between research and staff development may effect changes.

The second explanation is that when polytechnics were in their infancy and devising their procedures, folk-lore assumed that their staff included a significantly lower proportion with higher degrees than in universities. This may have led to a strong bias towards the acquisition of qualifications as a way of proving equal academic competence and comparable status. Whether any imbalance which may have existed, real or imagined, has been rectified by this approach is a matter worthy of study. Thirdly the funding system of polytechnics (outside London) imposes little financial strain on institutions if staff attend courses, since in many cases costs are met through the teacher training 'pool'. Research and return to practice do not qualify and must be met directly from institutional budgets. This support to attend courses may partly explain the longer average period of leave in polytechnics, since most full-time post-graduate courses require a year's leave whereas shorter periods of leave are suitable for other purposes.

Although it is unusual for universities or polytechnics to have formally approved policies on staff development, they usually have procedures for the award of leave. If leave contributes implicitly to staff development, individual staff and the institutions might benefit from more explicit consideration of the objectives and process of staff development.

The full results of this survey of staff development policies in British universities and polytechnics is expected to be published by SRHE in 1977.

FIGURE 1

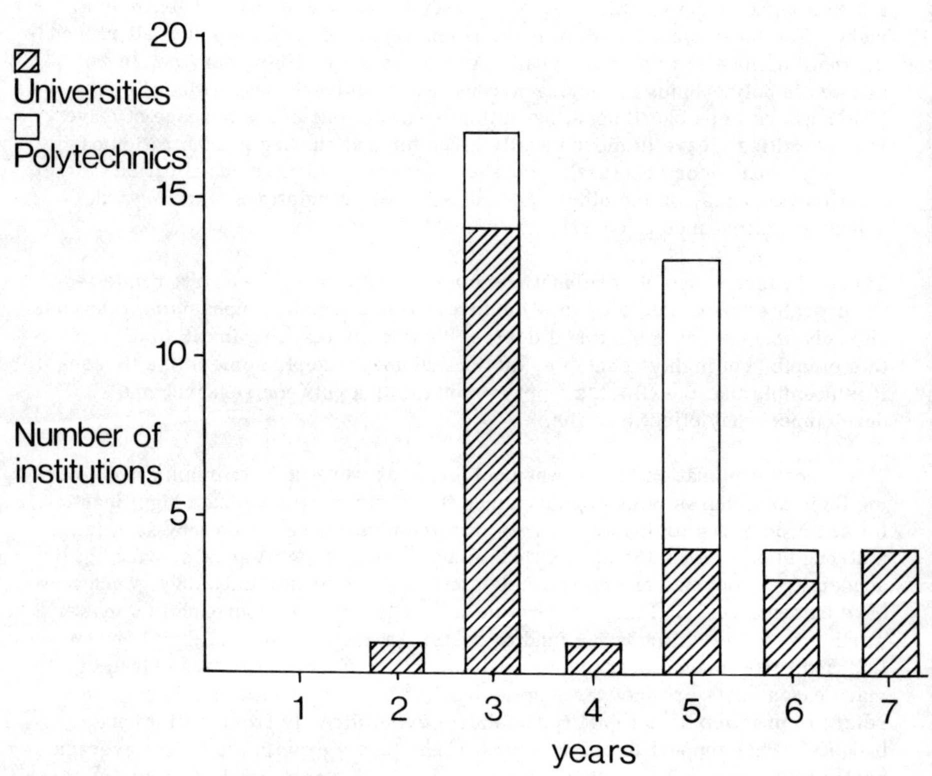

FIGURE 2

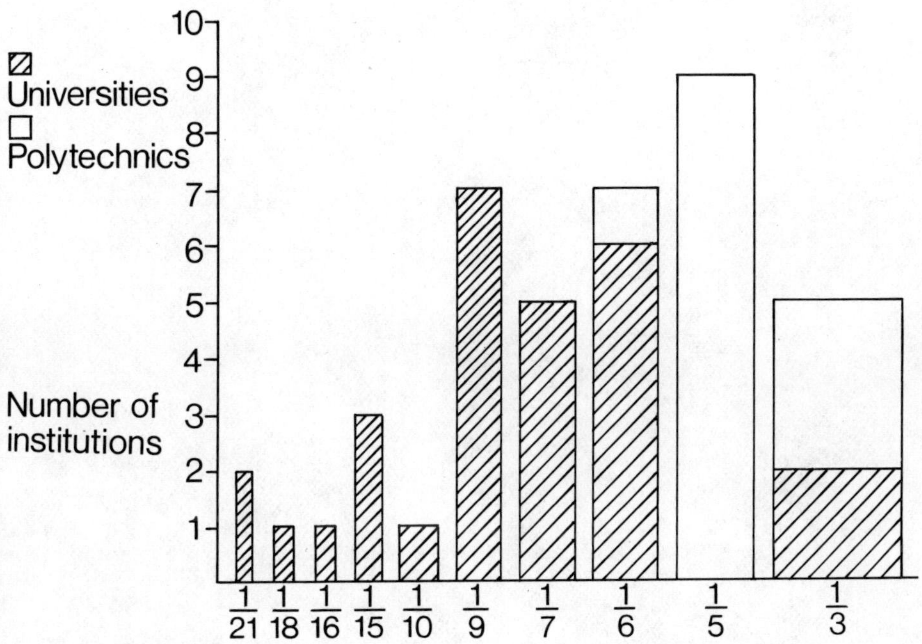
Proportion of service allowable as leave
Universities
Polytechnics
Number of institutions
10
9
8
7
6
5
4
3
2
1
1/21
1/18
1/16
1/15
1/10
1/9
1/7
1/6
1/5
1/3

7. SMALL GROUPS AND STAFF DEVELOPMENT

Staff Development Through and For Small Group Teaching

Mrs. M. L. J. Abercrombie

Small Group Work in University Staff Development

Professor Dr. B. Eckstein (Technische Hochschule, Aachen)

Tutorial Teaching in Science: The Experience of the H. E. L. P. Project

Professor P. J. Black, with J. Bliss and J. M. Ogborn (Chelsea College), B. K. Hodgson (Open University) and P. Unsworth (University of Sussex)

STAFF DEVELOPMENT THROUGH AND FOR SMALL GROUP TEACHING

by M. L. J. Abercrombie

This account is based on the work Paul Terry and I did in a project on improving small group teaching sponsored by the University Grants Committee 1972-75.

Our special interest is in interactive group discussion, in which emphasis is put on communication between students. Many valuable kinds of small group teaching do not depend on this, but for certain teaching objectives, e. g. encouraging autonomous learning, interactive groups are specially useful. Even if they have the wish and intention to run such classes, some teachers find difficulties in doing so, because they themselves have not been taught this way, and have no model on which to base effective behaviour. The models they automatically use are those of lectures, tutorials, seminars, practical classes whose objectives are mainly (though not always explicitly so) the transmission of a body of knowledge and skills. For this purpose the preferred channel of communication is between teacher and taught. This tends to strengthen the authority-dependency relationship which needs to be weakened if the intention is to encourage communication between peers. A different teaching style is required, and our aim was to strengthen personal aptitudes for this kind of work so that each participant became better able to develop his own methods appropriate to particular requirements, circumstances and potentialities.

Three main approaches were adopted:

a) Weekly meetings were held of small groups of teachers, from different disciplines and institutions, discussing their current small group teaching. The intention was to give them personal experience of learning by peer-interaction. As conductors, we aimed to establish a supportive climate in which, by comparison and contrast of his own behaviour with that of his peers, each participant could become aware of his own habitual ways of behaving. If these were not producing the effects he wanted, he could try out alternatives in his next class, and discuss outcomes in later meetings. Most of the issues that arose centred round the problems of relations with students. A discussion on naming illustrated the extraordinary range of behaviour among teachers, showing differences in basic assumptions about personal relationships, and reflecting the recent rapid changes in social custom. Some preferred Christian-naming, others found this embarrassingly familiar; some preferred asymmetry in mode of address, other were for strict equality, whether formal or informal; one never addressed students by name, another made a point of interviewing each student in order to get acquainted on an individual basis before starting group teaching. Other common topics were, how to get students to prepare for classes; problems of controlling content (covering the syllabus) and controlling participation (how to deal with the too talkative student, or silent one), and the effects of assessment on relationship. Some themes were concerned with general aims of higher education — to ensure that students pass examinations? or to develop the whole man? And some were about personal motivations for teaching.

b) Discussions about video recordings of their classes with teacher and students concerned. Perhaps the most striking phenomenon that became clear was the tendency for unconscious collusion to occur between students and teachers which defeated their declared objectives. Students who said they preferred active discussion to didactic teaching did not always prepare themselves adequately for it by reading the prescribed text. The teacher, in order to ensure that there was something to talk about, would respond by giving a summary of it, which signified that preparation on their part was redundant. The summary needed to be presented in a clear, concise and logical form, most efficiently as an unbroken monologue, whose smooth perfection made switching to hesitant, clumsy, questioning and self-exposing interactive discussion very difficult. Again, though it is generally accepted that one objective of discussion groups is to help all students to express themselves, teacher and students would collaborate in keeping the verbally fluent student dominant, and the shy one mute. It could be seen that the teacher, anxious to keep the party going, tacitly encouraged the student who did have something to say and could say it well, to engage with him in a dialogue. Signs that a silent member might be trying to speak were not perceived; the rest of the class gave up effort to join in. Studying the tape (this is quite a time-consuming process) enabled teacher and students to become sensitive to the verbal and non-verbal clues that had influenced their behaviour. Students decided to take more personal responsibility for controlling content and participation.

c) For large audiences, Paul Terry conducted discussions stimulated by the showing of excerpts from videotapes made for the purpose from (1) and (2). Some members of the audience readily empathized with teachers and students in the films and analysed situations portrayed in terms of their own experiences. This activity was most successful when run as a short course of four or so weekly meetings, during which a climate of confidence could develop. When 'one-off' shows were given, whether as an isolated event or as part of a conference, personal reactions to the general context might affect responses to the presentation.

A questionnaire was sent to 94 teachers (all the participants whose addresses we had) of whom 58 responded. Over three-fifths reported improvements in their small group teaching, and about one-tenth no change. Nearly three-fifths reported changes in other aspects of teaching, half of these in lecturing. Over a third reported improved relationships with students, and a quarter with colleagues.

It will be apparent that interactive group discussion offers a challenge to established authority-dependency relationships. Some of the difficulties in using interactive discussion about small group teaching to help teachers to come to terms with this basis change is the sharp variation in appetite for self-analysis. Some teachers were disappointed with our interactive approach and wanted straightforward teaching from us. At the other pole were a few who were disappointed that we did not subject them to a frankly psychotherapeutic method of changing their attitudes, e.g. with 't' or 'sensitivity group' methods. Fortunately there is room for many different personal approaches in teaching and learning.

Reference

ABERCROMBIE, M. L. J. and TERRY, P. M. Talking to Learn: improving teaching and learning in small groups to be published by SRHE, 1977

SMALL GROUP WORK IN UNIVERSITY STAFF DEVELOPMENT

by Brigitte Eckstein, Technische Hochschule Aachen, West Germany

Introduction

Experience over a number of years with training university teachers for teaching has shown that they frequently regard such training as essentially a matter of information transfer and the acquisition of certain teaching skills. When we take into account the low esteem in which teaching is generally held in universities in comparison with research, such an attitude to teacher training should cause no surprise.

However, student learning depends on the overall learning climate, which includes emotional factors as well as efficient information transfer. Hence, important as the command of teaching skills and knowledge are, they hardly compensate for a possible lack of interest in and concern for the students on the part of the teacher. In fact, if a teacher lacks true concern for his students, then participation in a training course with its resulting improvement in his teaching skills, may make him even more certain than he was before that a student's failure to learn must be the student's fault and not his.

On the other hand, a teacher who really cares for his students will continue to be aware of his own deficiencies as a teacher and strive to overcome them. Thus in addition to conveying teaching skills and knowledge of, for instance, learning psychology and educational theory, the training of university teachers is a matter of establishing or even changing attitudes.

Staff Training as a Threat

Thus staff training involves attitudinal, i.e. social, aims as well as cognitive ones. Now attitudinal aims can rarely be achieved through cognitive methods, such as for instance, exposing teachers to lectures in learning psychology. Instead, staff trainers have used group methods, which are known to be frequently effective in changing attitudes. However, any attempt at changing attitudes, especially basic ones, is generally experienced as a threat and thus tends to meet strong resistance. Special courses on group methods in teaching attract only a very small minority of teachers; they are a service for the converted, and on the average teacher have either an adverse impact or no impact at all. When the same methods are used to train the teachers, they are generally regarded with distrust and rejection.

A First Approach to Training through Groups

An approach that has been found much more acceptable is to start cognitively, using a conventional teaching method, and to use the group to discuss the material that has been learnt cognitively. The cognitive part may be a lecture or a demonstration such as a trigger film; at a later stage of the course self-instructional methods may be used. Alternatively, one can start with training in some skill, such as the preparation of audio-visual aids in a workshop or the production by the participants of an instructional videotape. The group discussion which follows any of these starters should in due course focus on the learning results achieved in the discussion and eventually the participants may be asked to consider under what circumstances they might offer this type of learning to their students. Such a discussion may even reveal some of the participants' basic attitudes to teaching, learning and students and lead — if necessary — to changes.

The advantage of this approach is that it carries hardly any risk and does not require special group dynamical competences on the part of the group tutor. Participants are confronted only very indirectly and lightly by their attitudes and beliefs and can easily escape self-confrontation altogether, so that attitudinal changes are generally moderate. They may be increased by video-recording the sessions and confronting participants with their own behaviour. However, this requires greater group dynamical competence in the tutor.

Abercrombie Sessions

Confronting the course participants with their attitudes and prejudices concerning teaching and learning, may be done by a concept developed and tested by Jane Abercrombie.[1] The participants of an 'Abercrombie-session' on higher education first get some stimulating material connected with controversial and biased educational topics — e.g. giftedness, student perception of teachers, non-directive teaching, aims and functions of the university, etc. The material (a trigger film, statistical material, a short text (about one page)) is first studied, and the participants are then asked to write down in 10 minutes its essential information content. After that, the matter is opened for discussion, without the facilitator (or any member) acting as chairman or formal discussion leader. The participants have to handle their own or other members' strive for dominance, to exert discipline and be aware of the demand of other members to speak. In the discussion, differences in perception and interpretation of the material and its content by the various participants become evident and can be focused on. Thus the underlying bias or attitude which led to this very perception of interpretation, and generally strongly related to the participants' actual ways of teaching, can be elucidated and, if need be, corrected.

Following this, the mutual actions and reactions in the group can be dealt with, and in particular, attitudes and behaviour can be exhibited in confrontation with ambiguous evidence or opposing opinions. The participants thus are confronted with their own prejudices concerning teaching, and with connected attitudes.

The approach thus offers a strong impact on basic attitudes, but it may be met by participants with strong emotional reactions, and even with refusal and resistances, especially when run by an inexperienced facilitator. Abercrombie sessions are no domain for the untrained group tutor!

A somewhat 'softer' approach based on the Abercrombie concept uses as a starting point for the discussion the different ways that teachers perceive and misperceive their students and possibly misinterpret their motives, e.g. mistaking fear or timidity as stupidity or even obstinacy. This approach has fewer risks, but offers poorer chances for changes of attitudes.

Abercrombie sessions may be included to a greater or lesser extent in any teaching and learning course.

Microteaching

A very useful approach which confronts teachers with their teaching attitudes has some resemblance to microteaching. The participants work in interdisciplinary groups of 12 to 14 members. They present short practice lectures or seminar sessions on a topic of their choice, prepared in advance of the course, which are video-recorded. They ought to last for 20 to 30 minutes, much longer than the sequences used in microteaching, which deal with skills rather than attitudes. The addressees of lecture or seminar are the other group members; a fictitious audience ('this lecture is part of a course for third year medical students!') is not acceptable. Thus the choice of topics is limited to basic matter, as most of the participants belong to other faculties, and have little pre-knowledge and sometimes not even any interest in the practice teacher's field. They thus offer a splendid simulation of a group of students with their variety of preknowledge, interest, and performance. In contrast to students however, the colleagues lectured are able and mostly willing to give the practice teacher thorough and frank feedback on his tuition, which he otherwise hardly ever gets.

This feedback is one of the central advantages of the method. A second is, that the participants during large parts of the sessions are in the very situation of student learners. Thus identifying with learners, they become sensitized to the students' needs, desires, fears, hopes, and problems. Being exposed to a dull lecture, they may realise what they perhaps habitually inflict on students. On the other hand, they may experience the possible fun and fascination of learning in a learner-centred setting and a group atmosphere of mutual trust, esteem, and co-operation, rather than in the more usual competitive situation.

After the lecture or seminar has been delivered, the group discusses the experience, focusing on 'how I felt being taught (or teaching) in this way?' The discussion may include technical topics of the presentation such as poor slides or overhead transparencies, poor audibility, a dull approach to the topic, or a misfit between assumed and actual preknowledge of the audience. Simultaneously the emotional aspects of learning are dealt with: How do I react emotionally to being lectured to (being 'instructed') ? [2] Do I feel just bored, or motivated to deal more thoroughly with the subject? Under what conditions might this seemingly dull topic gain my interest?

The videotape or its most essential part is then played back, and this provides material for a more detailed discussion, or for a more intense way of dealing with teacher's and audience's non-verbal signals. Altogether, one practice lecture can be delivered and dealt with in one 90-minute session. Additional sessions may be devoted to information and discussion on topics raised during the sessions. In addition, after several sessions the 'group process' — the mutual actions, reactions, and behaviour of the participants — may be dealt with through suitable parts of the videotaped group discussions. Members thus are confronted with their tendency to aggression or withdrawal, to dominance or submission, to mutual competition or to co-operation. In this way, the sequence of direct experience and subsequent theoretical interpretation, provides an introduction into basic group psychology through an unconventional teaching strategy. With more rigid participants, the facilitator will be wise to confine himself to just some hints regarding the group process and the members' typical behaviour, rather than actually focusing on it and possibly rousing resistances.

This method may again be offered as a course on its own, or included in a more comprehensive teaching-and-learning course. It can be adapted to the needs and conditions of the most diverse participants, either stressing the more technical or the more experiential side, according to the members' willingness. It produces a strong impact not only on actual teaching behaviour, but also on the teacher's basic assumptions of self, institution, students, and teaching and learning. A more direct training in communication and co-operation, in conflict solving and decision making, using mostly special group dynamical exercises, may or may not be included.

Conclusion

The methods described in this paper which emphasise the experiential side of teaching and learning, provide an opportunity to become aware of and to regard students, one's colleagues and oneself, as human beings owning emotions, hopes, and fears, as well as an intellect. On the other hand, realising students and colleagues to be real humans, might to some teachers seem frightening or even disgusting. The group sessions thus ought to offer mental support to participants who distrust their own ability to deal with a person as a person, and to make them aware of the ample rewards of being a whole and live person, even as a teacher. [2]

An essential part of university staff development ought to be concerned with the adaptability of university personnel to the accelerating changes in social and technical conditions. The university and its goals have to adapt to a varied and varying reality and to the new demands on university graduates, such as self- and peer-instruction, interdisciplinary co-operation and communication, and social responsibility. The necessity for change which thoroughly affects a person's identity is widely experienced as frightening. However, if we do not succeed in overcoming our anxieties and resistances to change, universities inevitably will become obsolete. Group work of the type described here has been tested with promising results. Evidently it may become an efficient tool in improving university teaching, and in the long run to safeguard universities against obsolescence.

References

1 ABERCROMBIE, M. L. J. (1969) Anatomy of Judgement Harmondsworth (Penguin paperback)

2 ROGERS, Carl R. (1969) Freedom to Learn Columbus, Ohio

TUTORIAL TEACHING IN SCIENCE – THE EXPERIENCE OF THE HELP PROJECT

by P.J. Black, J. Bliss, J.M. Ogborn, Centre for Science Education, Chelsea College, B.K. Hodgson, Open University, and P. Unsworth, University of Sussex

This paper describes results of work done in co-operation between staff in the physics departments of several universities and polytechnics as part of the HELP (Higher Education Learning Project in Physics) project.

The group has studied the problems of small group teaching in physics, by exchanging opinions and collecting evidence, by producing and testing materials for new types of small group teaching and by running two-day workshops for experienced staff. The main conclusions of the work will be published as a book intended for science teachers in higher education: this present paper will include a survey of this book concentrating on those features which are new.[1] The book is in three main parts, and it is suggested that any staff training or development should be in three corresponding stages.

It is important to base any approach to teachers on experience, to open up the private world of tutorial and to make clear that, both in appearance and in reality, any advice or analysis is based on experience. Narrative fiction, accounts written by tutors of particular tutorials, audio and video recordings have all been used. Study of such materials can help tutors to realise several important lessons. The first is that most colleagues experience the same difficulties as they do. A second lesson is that each intervention or reaction by a tutor helps both to define the character of personal relationships in the group, and to steer the group's progress; examples can show how short-term decisions have long-term effects which may be neither anticipated nor desired by the tutor. Appreciation of these effects lends powerful weight to the arguments for planning and preparation so that the outcome of tutorials can be better controlled, but it also shows that even the best preparations can be frustrated without careful thought about one's reactions on the spot. These points may be illustrated by some extracts from written accounts and transcripts and the ways in which suitable material may be collected and used in training tutors will be discussed.

The second stage of the approach is to analyse various aspects of the tutorial situation. A first aspect is an analysis of the various possible aims for tutorial teaching. Different aims can compete or conflict and one value of an analysis is to help the tutor to clarify his own priorities. A second aspect is the study of personal and group interactions and the various features, seating, posture, eye contact and so on which affect their development. Both of these will be discussed briefly, and more attention will be devoted to a third aspect where the project's work makes some new points. This aspect concerns verbal transactions: the study of transcripts gives striking evidence of the many contrasts between the talk of tutors and of students. This study emphasises the patience and care needed for encouraging student talk. A particular aspect of importance is the way in which tutors ask questions and the various styles and types of questions have been reviewed. The changes needed to encourage student talk do not amount to putting the same point in a different way: they necessarily lead to a reappraisal of the tutor's image of what a good tutorial may achieve — one difficulty explored and discussed may take the time of five 'explanations'.

The third stage concentrates on planning and preparation, under three main aspects. One aspect is the possibility of a negotiated contract between a tutor and his students about the group's method of working.

A second aspect is the use of prepared outlines which specify both a task, with concrete examples, and a procedure. Examples of outlines, prepared and tested within the project, will be given. Some are for the conventional tutorial, others are more suitable for larger groups using a routine of work in small sub-groups which report back and compare their conclusions. These materials may be particularly suitable for training students in some cognitive skills, a feature which raises a question about aims — whether tutorial teaching in science is a secondary activity, to help the student with the primary 'courses', or whether it should be the primary method for certain aims of a degree course. One need in any training is to provide experience and help in preparation of suitable materials for work of this type.

A third main aspect is the possibility of thinking more clearly about one's strategy for tutorials, and of realising aims by a planned sequence of tutorials, using prepared outlines and procedures for some of them. Examples of such strategies will be presented.

The broader relevance of the study to tutorials in faculties other than science will be reviewed and the applications of its findings in staff development and training will be discussed.

Reference

OGBORN, J. (editor) (1977) Small Group Teaching in Undergraduate Science London, Heinemann Educational Books

8. PRACTICAL MODELS

A SELF-TUITION UNIT FOR UNIVERSITY STAFF DEVELOPMENT

by N. C. Boreham, Department of Adult and Higher Education, University of Manchester, and Pamela Richmond, Audio-Visual Service, University of Manchester

The Staff Teaching Workshop at Manchester University provides opportunities for lecturers to obtain information about educational media and methods, develop their teaching skill, and evaluate their own teaching effectiveness. The Workshop, which occupies a large room on two levels, is open for most of the year, and continuous cover is provided by one full-time staff member. Emphasis in the Workshop is placed on self-tuition: there are no formal courses. Lecturers can visit the Workshop when they want to improve their teaching, and the role of the staff is primarily to facilitate a process of learning through discovery.

The simplest service provided is to give information about teaching methods and to demonstrate teaching aids. However, there is also a preparation area in which lecturers can plan their teaching and make their own audio-visual aids. Although facilities are provided elsewhere in the University for the production of slides, transparencies etc. to order, 'do-it-yourself' activities in the Workshop enable lecturers to experiment before committing themselves to a particular approach, and enable them to learn the potential and the limitations of different techniques. The third service provided is the evaluation of teaching. At their own request, lecturers can be videotaped and counselled, helped in the drafting of evaluation questionnaires, and assisted with educational research.

The Workshop exists to improve lecturers' teaching effectiveness. However, its approach is essentially non-directive. How the Workshop is used depends on how the individual lecturer wishes to use it, and it is he who takes all the major initiatives. The kind of learning experience provided in the Workshop can be described thus:

a) It is initiated by the lecturer himself — arising from his own perception of a need to do something about his teaching.

b) It is active and self-directed: teaching duties for Workshop staff are to act as a sounding board for the lecturers' suggestions, proposals and ideas, and facilitate an effective learning experience by making equipment and information available.

c) It is on-line. Although the Workshop is situated in a non-teaching building, ease of access enables lecturers to visit it in the course of preparing their lectures.

It is too soon to attempt a summative evaluation of this approach to university staff development. Nevertheless, the Workshop has been favourably received, and there is evidence that it has had an impact on teaching effectiveness. This is in contrast to the more conventional courses in teaching method, which are viewed with hostility by some university lecturers, and judged irrelevant to their needs by some others. We suggest that these negative reactions to the traditional type of course can be related to the following factors:

a) The menu of learning experiences is decided mainly by the course organisers, not by the participants.

b) Learning is off-the-job: courses are usually arranged before the session begins, or during a vacation.

Both these features tend to distance the learning experience from the transfer task — the first conceptually, the second temporally.

c) The learning experiences provided on the conventional course are frequently didactic: participants file into a hall and listen to an expert.

This feature tends to create hostility. Lecturers are cast in the role of students, and yet the expert who lectures them is usually not an expert in <u>their</u> field.

An evaluation of the Staff Teaching Workshop would begin by pointing out that it is on these three points that the Workshop departs from the conventional type of course. We suggest (but cannot prove) that initiation of the learning experience by the participants, provision of on-line facilities for developing teaching skills, and active self-directed learning, result in greater relevance to lecturers' needs and reduced hostility to the idea of learning how to teach more effectively. This is not to suggest that the Workshop approach is better than the conventional type of course. However, it seems to have a valuable complementary role to play in university staff development.

ONTARIO'S FIRST MAJOR WORKSHOP FOR UNIVERSITY TEACHERS

by Frederick W. Parrett, Director, Ontario Universities Program for Instructional Development at Queen's University, Kingston, Ontario

An organised province-wide commitment to instructional development began with the establishment of an 'Ontario Universities Program for Instructional Development' in July 1973 after considerable discussion at senior provincial government and university levels on how the proposed programme should function. Initially, the Programme was a small grand-awarding body with a limited commitment and viability with respect to organising workshops and dealing with information dissemination.

After three years, which one might describe as 'up and down', the Programme has evolved and shifted away from a small-grant function to an institutional-grant concept with considerably more emphasis on 'staff' workshops and on information disbursement.

In May 1976 the Programme sponsored the first one-week workshop for university teachers at which some 35 university professors of various disciplines and teaching experience met to work intensively on improving their teaching skills. Details of this most successful workshop were described. One workshop per year such as this cannot hope to fulfil the needs of all the university teachers in Ontario (approximately 40 per cent of all Canada's faculty and students are in the 15 universities in the Province of Ontario). Indeed, the long-term objective of the province-wide programme is to ensure the continued and visible commitment to improving teaching and learning at an individual university level, and when a university has made little organised effort in this direction, to encourage its development. Province-wide workshops for university teachers on improving teaching skills will not be sufficient to achieve this objective; therefore, another aspect of the Programme's work is to train more 'leaders' who can operate at a local campus level.

An example of this are two workshops held in August 1976, which we call 'Workshops on Designing Workshops', one each on lecturing and small group teaching. Participants in these workshops signed a 'contract' that they will take the workshop they have designed in co-operation with other delegates back to their own universities and run them for the benefit of their colleagues. Reports and material from these workshops were distributed.

It is hoped that meetings of the latter type will initiate a 'chain reaction' which will significantly increase the number of resource persons and increase the awareness throughout the province as to where they can obtain experienced assistance if it is needed in developing their own programmes or units.

THE CASE FOR NEED-ORIENTED, TRAINEE-DIRECTED COURSES OF TRAINING

by John Cowan, Civil Engineering Learning Unit, Heriot-Watt University

A Personal Introduction

I think the most effective training course I ever attended was one which my Mother ran for me when I was a wee boy. It was a 'house-training' course, which had a very clearly defined goal; and I can vouch for the fact that the training programme was both rigorous and thorough, and that the need for training went unquestioned by all concerned. Please remember these three points, because I think they are relevant to my topic.

Some years later, in common with many other Scots of my generation, I went on a different kind of training, where I encountered a military gentleman with a loud voice who trained me, in a number of basic skills. Here again the training programme was rigorous, the goals clearly defined — and trainees were never permitted to question the need for the stipulated terminal behaviour.

Some years later I ended up in the construction industry, where I had to go aloft to supervise steel erectors on high structures. Fortunately someone was foresighted enough to give me sufficient rudimentary training to save me from making several unrepeatable slips. Once again you can appreciate that the training goals were clearly defined, the programme thorough, though brief, and the need for training indisputable.

I would submit that these three characteristics which I have been emphasising are to be found in most successful training schemes — until we come to look at the training of university teachers.

For, looking back over the best of such courses that I have attended the first thing I always remember is that a fair number of participants seemed to be constantly bickering about the need, if any, for the training which was being offered to them. The discipline was generally far from rigorous while, as for the goals of the courses, I doubt if any group of assembled participants could ever have agreed on a unanimous statement of their specific expectations. Notice, then, that lecturer training is far from conforming to my list of three characteristics of effective training courses.

That introduction brings me, somewhat circuitously I'm afraid, to the first point in the paper. I will now try to be less personal, and more succinct.

Training University Teachers

The 'training' of university teachers in 1976 is unlike any other recognised form of training. Indeed, it might be more helpful to describe it, metaphorically, as if it were a kind of preparation for a journey into the unknown. A small group of interested recruits are taken temporarily from a heathen society which worships the twin gods of research and consultancy, and which knows little of the one true god of education. These novices are briefly indoctrinated with a gospel of commitment to student learning in a more meanginful form. Then, without even having been dried behind their ears, they are sent back to their homeland, where they now find that the treatment they have received has made them misfits. They seem to their colleagues to have acquired angelic tendencies, for they are always up in the air, harping on about their new ideas and innovations. But quickly the balloon is pricked; because they founder on the rock-firm resistance of more mature colleagues who know, from the background of their long experience, that what they've been doing (or not doing) in the past must always continue to be the right approach for everyone.

But any training which an active lecturer receives is surely a pointless exercise unless it improves or modifies or enriches or extends the scope of his contribution to student learning. It may achieve this by improving or developing an ability or skill, or by teaching him a new skill. Or alternatively a training course may deliberately set out to help him to restate his aims and methods. But at the end of the day, the training of a university teacher is not a meaningful exercise unless changes are then brought about, by the teacher concerned, in his sector or his departmental environment. And that's the second point in this paper, which, if it's true, has important implications.

The Home Environment

Consider the diagram shown in Figure 1 (p. 117), where everything inside the circle represents the departmental environment. If our embryo trainee is already a member of that department, then parts of his life (such as his religious beliefs, his hobbies, and his family) will lie completely outwith the scope of what happens in his department. So it is only that part lying within the sector which concerns us here. If our lecturer goes off on a training course, he will presumably develop certain abilities, and perhaps may decide that he should let others atrophy somewhat. So he's not quite the same chap anymore (Figure 2, p. 117); and as soon as he gets back to his home department, it quickly becomes apparent that he doesn't fit in properly or easily (Figure 3, p. 117). Some of those corners will at least have to be rubbed off before he can be integrated into the life of the department again. And if by any chance he has thought so hard about the aims of higher education that he has also changed his standpoint (Figure 4, p. 117), then his assimilation back into his home environment will be even more difficult.

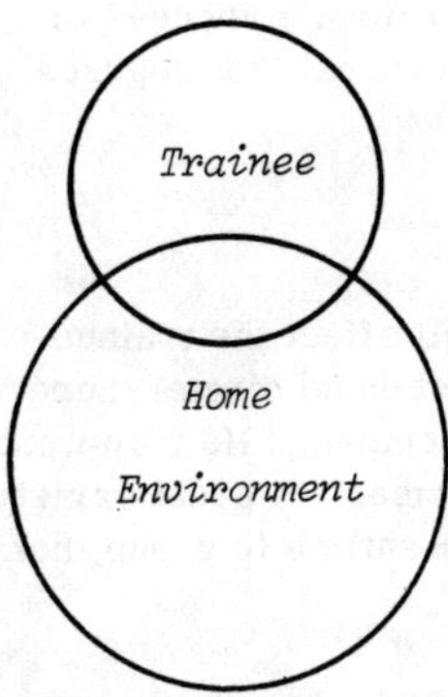

Fig 1

The Trainee and his environment

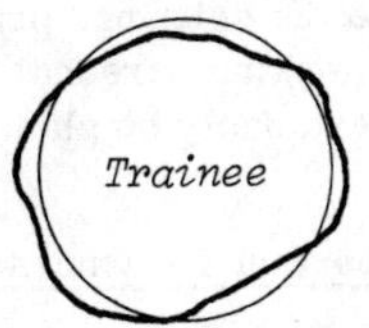

Fig 2

Changes in Trainee

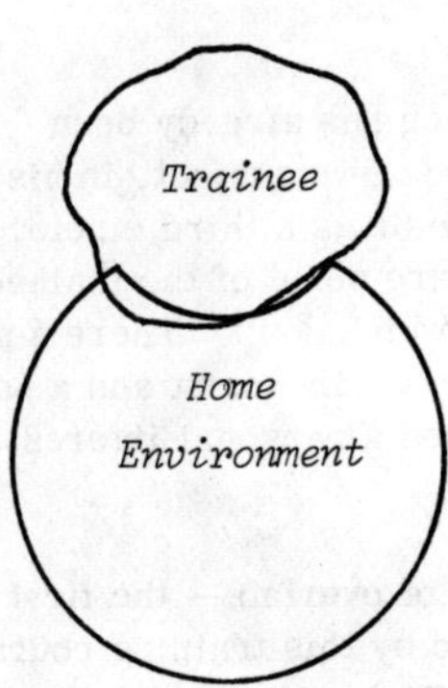

Fig 3

An imperfect fit

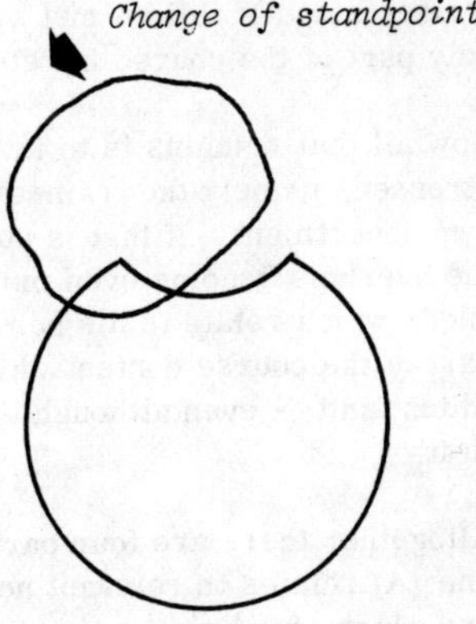

Fig 4

Effect of Change of standpoint

Point three, then, is that, if changes resulting from training are related so directly to the existing, practical environment, then the trainee's success or failure in making personal and other changes there is so critical that courses should presumably be planned on that basis.

Other Important Influences on Course Structure

There are at least three groups of factors which could well affect the trainee significantly (Figure 5, p. 119). First of all (in the top left-hand circle) there are his own personal needs, both known and as yet undetermined. He may want to learn how to run seminars, or how to plan design exercises. A great variety of possible needs could be suggested but it is sufficient meantime to group them all together.

The next grouping (in the top right-hand circle of Figure 5) is the course content which is being offered, formally or informally, during the period of training. If, for instance, it happens to be a course which deals specifically with the use of CCTV in teaching which is exactly what our trainee thinks he wants to learn, the contents of the course will still almost inevitably include some items which relate to the use and maintenance of the equipment (which may not interest him), some which relate to production problems (which his subject field is unlikely to generate), some items which he may not have the background knowledge to understand, and some items which he knows about already, because of his previous interest in the subject. When these two groups are considered together (Figure 6, p. 119) one can see from the overlap that only a part of this particular trainee's needs will be met by this particular course; so he will consider that only part of the course is relevant to his needs.

Now all that remains is to introduce the third factor which has already been stressed, namely the trainee's particular situation, in his own subject, in his own department. If that is put on to the diagram (Figure 6) as a third circle, the overlaps become even more interesting. For there are some of the trainee's needs which relate to his home environment, and some which don't. There's a part of the course content which is relevant for his home environment and a part which isn't — even although the trainee may have declared a personal interest in it.

Altogether there are four particularly interesting areas of overlap — the first one (A) relates to relevant needs which won't be covered by this training course, and which, for brevity might well be called 'untaught'. The next (B) is for course material which satisfied the demand from the trainee, but is of no direct relevance to his home environment — so it's really 'enrichment' material. The next area (C) is a more difficult one; it includes topics in the training course which do relate to the home environment, but not to the trainee's role there; perhaps that sector is best titled 'familiarisation'. Finally in the middle (D), there is the small core of 'vital' material which indisputably belong to all three groupings.

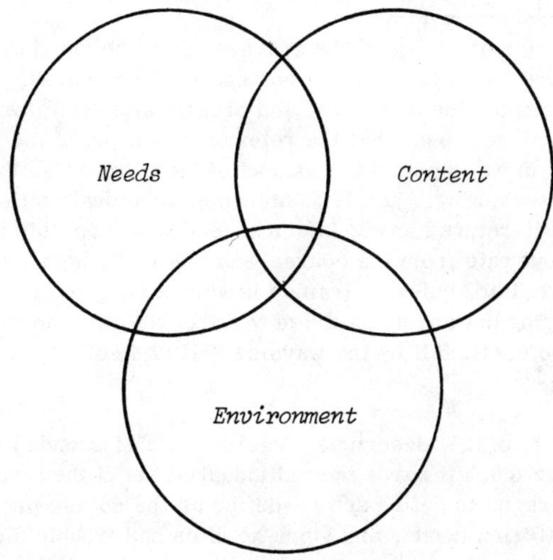
Needs
Content
Environment

Fig 5

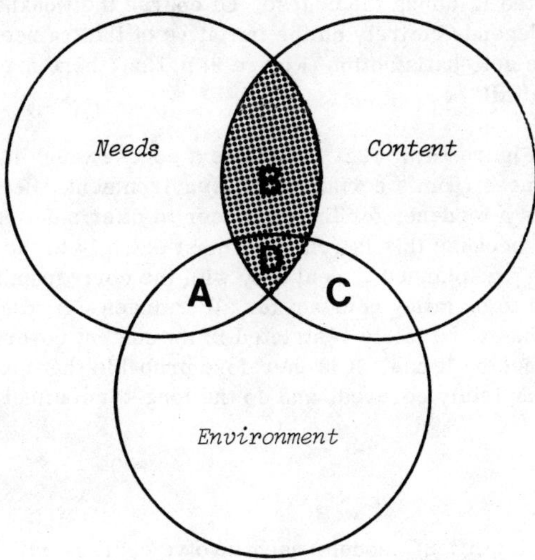
Needs
Content
B
D
A
C
Environment

Fig 6

Using This Descriptive Approach

I have attempted to classify a few of the courses I have attended by relating them to this model: Figure 7 (p. 121) shows a content-centred course, where the organisers predetermined the objectives and programme within well-defined limits. Sadly the trainees found that the relevance of much of the material was questionable. But a more important weakness of the course was the relatively large 'untaught' part which was just left untouched to be dealt with by the trainees, on their own, on their return home. Informal feedback from this group suggested that the final drop-out rate from the course was tragically high! And is that not only to be expected? For, unless a trainee is very strong willed, the important stage of actually trying out and using the new skill or ability, in regular service teaching, can all too easily fall by the wayside if it is a solitary and unassisted activity.

In contrast, Figure 8 (p. 121) describes a course which I attended recently. This one was slanted very much towards the individual needs of the trainees, which they were all encouraged to define and re-define as the course proceeded. Since each trainee had differing needs, and since he often had trouble distinguishing them, the limits of the course content were a little vague and the coverage was probably patchy. But the trainees naturally selfish concerns with their own problems, as they discerned them, meant that, for each individual, there was a fair coverage of his personal 'untaught' sector, and they all made sure that there was adequate follow-up because they were in charge of it themselves, and had planned it and initiated it during the course. Of course the weakness of such an approach is that it depends entirely on the initiative of the trainee. If he defines his needs with undue self-satisfaction (Figure 9, p. 122) there may be no overlaps to be filled in at all!

The final example (Figure 10, p. 122) describes a course which is intended specifically for trainees from a certain type of environment. Because of that structuring, there is a tendency for the organiser to offer a deliberately restricted course-content, because this is related almost entirely to the chosen home environment, and is pre-planned to deal only with the corresponding needs, which are presumed to be fairly constant for all trainees. By reason of its design, this model has to be fairly restricted in its content coverage, or else it may lose what cohesion it has. It is therefore probable that the possible content will be incompletely covered, and so the long-term effect may be equally limited.

Summary

These three (over-simplified) models each involve courses with different emphases.

When the subject matter of the course is the top priority, there is so much to cover with a mixed target population that the amount of subject matter which will be directly suitable in any one home environment will be sparse. So the trainee

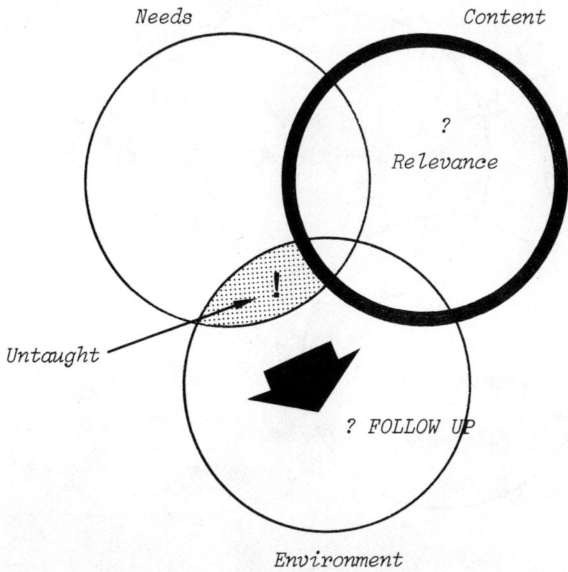

Fig 7

Content Centred Course

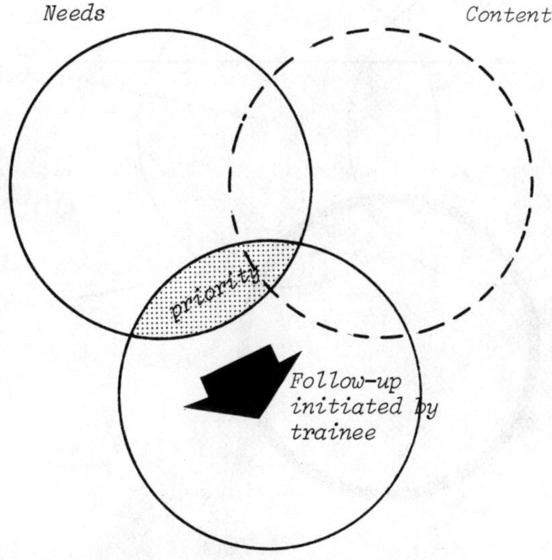

Fig 8

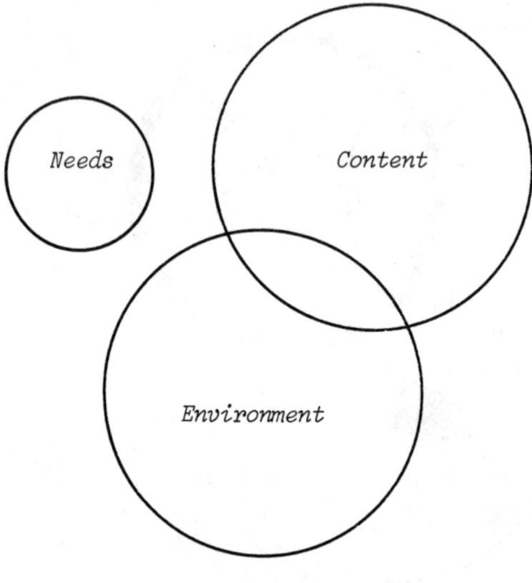
Needs
Content
Environment

Fig 9

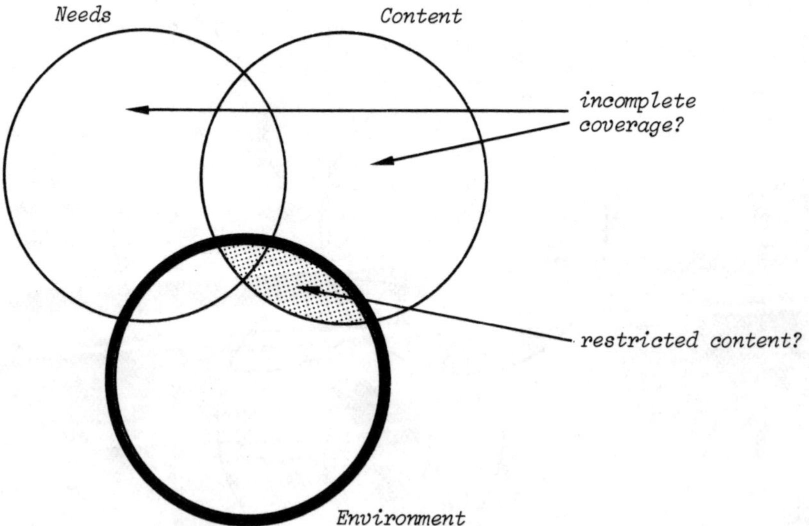
Needs
Content
incomplete
coverage?
restricted content?
Environment

Fig 10

will still have to discover for himself how to apply these new techniques in his own situation.

The same problem faces the trainee in a context-based course, where in a sense he suffers from the disadvantage of an over-sympathetic and over-specialised training situation. The situation is inward looking; the trainee does not have to serve with those who are not like-minded, and to plan with those who have other aims in mind. Again, that hurdle is left to the follow-up stage, by which time the trainee is (once again) on his own, and relatively unprepared.

The reader will have gathered that my own preference in all of this is for a course during which I can start to relate the new philosophy, or whatever it is, to my home environment. This can be arranged when the needs of each individual are made the priority; for the initiative remains to a great extent with the individual. Time can be (and usually is) spent on needs which do not relate to the home situation, when these are important to the trainee. But follow-up and implementation can be safely left with the individual, and their success will depend on his continuing ability to sustain enthusiasm and motivation; though speaking quite selfishly as a trainee, I would dearly like to see some kind of a sustained follow-up and back-up.

I would therefore campaign for a need-oriented, trainee-directed training programme, rather than an isolated training course. In this there should be a strong emphasis on the integration of new skills and attitudes in the home situation, with some kind of a continuing and supportive contact while that is happening.

A Personal Afterthought

Having been given the chance to express my viewpoints, I would like to add here that, for the life of me, I don't understand how so many people can presently run training courses without feedback. They don't know for sure, or in detail, how we get on once we go back to our departments; so how can they go on and train any more of us lecturers, until they get that feedback?

9. WORKSHOPS

Exercises and Occasions: Practical Course and Class Design

Professor J. Broadbent (University of East Anglia)

Senate in Action: An Experience in Workshop Development

L. F. Evans (The City University)

There are Many Ways of Teaching Grandmothers to Suck Eggs

J. A. Riley (Open University)

The Use of 'Trigger' Films in Developing Teaching Skills

Dr. J. P. Powell (University of New South Wales)

Staff Development Activities at the University of Sussex

Dr. M. Eraut, with B. Connors, E. Hewton, A. Horton and C. Miller (University of Sussex)

Sexaboard: An Examination Board Simulation Game

Dr. S. Armstrong, with J. Cable, T. J. Gaskell (Huddersfield Polytechnic)

Repertory Grid Techniques Applied to the Identification of Aspects of Pedagogic Style Contributing to Teacher Effectiveness

T. R. Keen (Plymouth Polytechnic)

Microteaching as an Analogue of Lecturing

Dr. G. Brown (University of Nottingham)

In the following section on the eight workshops run during the Conference, the report of the presenter of each workshop is printed on the left-hand side of the page, faced by a report of one of the participants (on the right-hand side of the page).

EXERCISES AND OCCASIONS: PRACTICAL COURSE AND CLASS DESIGN

by John Broadbent, University of East Anglia

"The task of the teacher is to provide exercises and occasions." [1]

A workshop whose members will be able to practise the design of courses/classes. Some propositions behind the workshop (further documentation was provided for discussion):

a) An occasion for learning about teaching should be a model for learning about any other subject: "sustaining the sensibility of a learner is probably more valuable to a teacher than any set of tips or techniques." [2]

b) "The problem for each teacher is to devise situations in which students are led to create for themselves sustained structures of thinking rather than merely trying to master extracts of prestructured subject matter." [3]

c) Teaching modes model other behaviours in society: "The truth about a society, it would seem, is to be found in the actual relations, always exceptionally complicated, between the system of decision, the system of communication and learning, the system of maintenance, and the system of generation and nurture." [4]

d) Therefore participatory modes are desirable.

e) They also reflect the mode in which knowledge is available to us: "Natural phenomena as now conceived by the sciences must be understood as a dynamic, a drama"; [5] "Most learning is not the result of instruction. It is rather the result of unhampered participation in a meaningful situation." [6]

f) To be most participatory, to tap the varied resources of students, our exercises and occasions should employ multiple modes, rather than consist of 'the lecture-course' or 'discussion' uniformly.

Notes and References

1 BRUNER, J. S. (1966) Towards a Theory of Instruction Harvard U. P.

2 GROUP FOR HUMAN DEVELOPMENT IN HIGHER EDUCATION (1974) Faculty Development in a Time of Retrenchment Change Publications

PARTICIPANT'S REPORT

by Vincent Worth, Open University

Professor Broadbent's presentation provided a useful opportunity to rethink and perhaps modify those ways of conducting class teaching which we take for granted in much of our everyday work.

After an introduction, the workshop was divided into sub-groups so that members could get to know each other and then to discuss extracts from the work of some selected writers on education which in one way or another constituted a justification for 'multi-modal' teaching and learning. 'Multi-modality' I took to mean the use of a range of teaching and learning which might include, for example, the conventional tutorial, the tutorless group, library exercises and so on; in Professor Broadbent's terms, 'varied and participatory and interactive'.

Lack of time prevented more than a brief discussion of these extracts and this was a serious though unavoidable weakness in the programme since some extended consideration of issues of principle was highly desirable before the group launched itself into practical concerns. It is, for example, relevant to note that one participant claimed to be using a multi-modal teaching strategy, but the justification for this was couched in psychological and operational terms rather than in the social and political reasons from which the workshop started. It would have been a fruitful exercise to consider 'multi-modality' using Bernstein's 'classification' and 'framing' as sensitising concepts.

After the brief discussion, the sub-groups were invited to plan a programme of work centred on 'multi-modality' as a pedagogic strategy. Again only the briefest of discussions was possible of the accounts given by two of the workshop group. However, some interesting points did emerge in the conclusion: what was touched on but could have been more fully explored, had time permitted, were the structural relationships between the different 'modes' and 'levels' and the total teaching and learning situation.

As a contribution to the idea and process of staff development the exercise was of considerable value in generating professional self-consciousness and a teaching strategy that, in the words of Professor Broadbent's handout, would 'tap the diversity of gifts of students (and staff), and... provide the optimal arousal for learning'.

3 CHANAN, G. and GILCHRIST, L. (1974) What School Is For Penguin

4 WILLIAMS, R. (1961) The Long Revolution Chatto

5 SCHWAB, J.J. (1962) The concept of the structure of a discipline. Reprinted in GLOCK, M.D. (editor) (1971) Guiding Learning: Readings in Educational Psychology

6 ILLICH, I. (1971) Deschooling Society

SENATE IN ACTION: AN EXPERIENCE IN WORKSHOP DEVELOPMENT

by L. F. Evans, The City University

The 'Conduct of Meetings' study and training project which received an earmarked grant from the U. G. C. as part of the 1971/72 Educational Developments programme, included provision for the video-recording and subsequent analysis of meetings in Universities, and the provision of training exercises based on that material. From the many recordings made, one particular episode, at a meeting of the Senate of The City University, provided a source of study which, supported with relevant documentation, enabled a useful training exercise to be devised.

The development of the exercise involved, initially, a repeated reviewing of the video-recording in order to abstract an incident which had an internal unity, in which a large number of participants contributed to the discussion, and in which matters such as the 'chairmanship', the nature of decision-making and recording, interaction among participants, and the physical arrangement of the room, could be studied. Having isolated such an incident, the Senate Agenda and relevant papers were reproduced and assembled to give an initial 'paper-reading' experience, before viewing the recording.

In its original form, the instructions to those taking part in the exercise gave a general indication of observations to be made and subsequent tasks to be carried out. As a result of the initial runs, the exercise was modified, to give a more 'time conscious' aspect to the paper reading, introducing also a short objective test to be completed before proceeding to the viewing phase.

The allocation of specific tasks within a 'viewing group' of six was found to be more effective than a general indication in the later modifications of the exercise, and the particular tasks were changed and enlarged as a result of 'feedback' from workshop participants.

The workshop experience offered at this Conference includes participation in the current version of the exercise, and discussion with the workshop director of its developmental aspects.

The earlier development and the '1974' version of the exercise is reported in 'Issues in Staff Development', an SDU/UTMU publication.

PARTICIPANT'S REPORT

by J. Cowan, Heriot-Watt University

Procedure

This was a Workshop about a workshop. Mr. Evans used his material, first of all, to let us experience the kind of situation which was faced by staff attending one of a number of activities at a training workshop for people who wished to perform better in meetings. The session therefore began with an explanation of the circumstances in which the material was used. Leo Evans did this in the effective and friendly way which we have come to expect from him, while at the same time gently introducing the participants to their neighbours in preparation for the next part of the programme.

We then had a condensed version of the workshop experience. We viewed a videotape of part of a meeting of a University senate, having first been briefed on what we would be required to do thereafter, and having been divided in to groups for that purpose. Each sub-group had a different task, which was only a small part of the brief that would have been handed to genuine workshop participants. However, it was sufficiently long to give us a taste of the atmosphere and the experience involved, and it served as a focus for the discussion which was to follow. We closed by considering the value of this sort of activity in a staff training programme.

Outcome

The material was extremely interesting and provocative. As a result some of the participants were understandably diverted into consideration and discussion of the issues which had involved the senate, or other extraneous matters, and had to be gently drawn back to the topic in hand. At a later stage in the proceedings we went on to ask questions about the collection and editing of the material, and the reaction of participants when it was used in a genuine workshop situation, which all seemed to indicate that those present saw the relevance of this sort of workshop training situation.

Comments

1) It would be easy to under-value the immense contribution which is made in this sort of activity by a very competent leader. The fact that Leo Evans played

his part unobtrusively may have meant that it was only on reflection that we realised how much the success of the workshop depended on him.

2) I already knew something of the senate workshop before I attended this particular meeting. Nevertheless it was only by participating in this 'Workshop about a workshop' that I really obtained an impression of the reactions of someone in such a workshop. It is difficult to suggest any other way of conveying that impression, other than by letting each participant experience it for himself.

3) It was clear from the evidence on the video-tape, and from the comments of the workshop participants, that inability to handle meetings or to take part in them adequately is a very common failing amongst university staff. Therefore the need for training to cover aspects other than lecturing ability was very clearly underlined.

THERE ARE MANY WAYS OF TEACHING GRANDMOTHERS TO SUCK EGGS

by J.A. Riley, Open University

This workshop was designed to allow its members to consider a wide range of different approaches to the development of the teaching abilities of staff in higher education. These approaches included a range of relatively didactic methods, such as lectures, providing written guidelines or programmed learning, and others, more informal, such as group exercises, quizzes, personal tutorials or feedback on effectiveness. There were opportunities to experience several of these approaches during the workshop and to consider their relative merits. The particular skill whose development was discussed was that of learning to write good multiple-choice questions.

There was also an exhibit showing some of our approaches to developing the skills of marking essays and of preparing material for students to study in their own time.

PARTICIPANT'S REPORT

by Chris Furedy, University of York, Canada

This session was designed to illustrate some of the ways in which staff can be aided to improve teaching techniques by the staff of teaching units. The principle assumption illustrated and discussed by the group, led by Judith Riley of the Open University, was that an experiential approach, which requires the staff member to work through a problem, will be preferable to merely supplying information. To put it simply, the university teacher, like any learner, can 'learn through doing'.

Ms. Riley illustrated her point by having the group complete a multiple-choice test to simulate the occasion when the staff member requests help in devising such tests. The group were actually given two somewhat different tests in order to emphasise the point that slight differences in item construction can lead to significant differences in students' scores. Other aspects of multiple-choice testing were discussed by the group. The experiential approach to teaching improvement was debated. The group was sympathetic to the approach but the point was made that it is rather time-consuming and some staff may prefer to receive information and make their own choices about how to utilise it in their teaching. Ms. Riley emphasised the importance of sensitivity and tact in making suggestions about how a staff member should teach a subject or assess students. She has experienced degrees of resistance to change on the part of staff who nevertheless perceived that their testing procedures could be improved.

The session made its point well, but the range of ways a grandmother can be taught to suck eggs could not be conveyed in a short session geared to experiencing the problems of constructing multiple-choice tests. The group, like many student discussion groups, became involved in the specific example so there was little time to pursue more general principles.

On a personal note, I thought that Ms. Riley illustrated through her enthusiasm, concern and pleasant manner some important characteristics of effective 'staff developers'.

THE USE OF 'TRIGGER' FILMS IN DEVELOPING TEACHING SKILLS

by J. P. Powell, Tertiary Education Research Centre, University of New South Wales

Film and videotape material has been used for a number of years at the University of N. S. W. in staff development workshops and seminars. A variety of material has been produced for this purpose, most of it being of the 'Trigger' film type. This consists of short episodes, two or three minutes in length, designed to stimulate discussion in small groups. Each episode presents a routine, problematic or emotion-laden situation which can then by analysed, commented upon or further developed by members of the group.

This material has been shown to be effective in generating discussion. It is highly realistic and makes an immediate impact, especially if the content includes emotional elements. The scenes are almost always problematic and open-ended so that members of the audience are encouraged to explore their own feelings and experiences in order to suggest a variety of solutions. Because of the 'distancing' effect of film the participants are less threatened than would be the case if role-playing or a re-play of a videotape of their own teaching were involved.

The major area of application has so far been in the development of interpersonal skills: training observational powers, increasing insight and empathy, promoting the ability to foresee possible consequences of actions, and facilitating prompt and appropriate responses in dynamic interpersonal situations. But there are a number of other applications of obvious relevance to the developing of other teaching skills such as displaying exemplars of particular techniques and providing a basis for role-playing.

PARTICIPANT'S REPORT

by Stuart Trickey, Department of Education Services, Sheffield City Polytechnic

I write this report as an enthusiastic user of Dr. Powell's first efforts at making trigger films in a teaching methods course for new polytechnic staff. These were 14-minute films in monochrome which present six or seven brief 'real-life' sequences aimed to prompt the viewer to re-examine attitudes and trigger discussion. One film dealt with teaching problems arising, broadly speaking, from lectures and the other from small group teaching.

Clips from these films were shown to the workshop audience. One trigger encounter showed an archetypal pompous lecturer, suitably irritating, in a post-lecture conversation with two disillusioned students. Out pops a gem, the epitome of his perception of his role: "My job is just to teach you the material. It is not my business to make you interested in it; you have to do that for yourselves". Another sequence showed a blackboard user at his appalling worst. With back to the audience he incoherently mutters while smearing the board with illegible meanderings. Within small group discussion we saw examples of the egocentric tutor, and skilful and less-than-skilful response probing.

Dr. Powell's new films — and there are as many as nine of these — are all in colour, which is a good deal more pleasing. The critical incidents are shorter than those in the first two films with some as brief as 20 seconds, and they illustrate aspects of teaching, management, nursing, medicine, social work and the public service. The band of actors, a paid troup of drama students, were starting to have familiar faces and this, together with some transparently contrived scenes of extreme brevity, tended to diminish the impact as time wore on. Trigger films are powerful tools to facilitate discussion, but it seems that the script, scene setting and acting need to reach professional standards; it seems too that $1\frac{1}{2}$-2 minute incidents are about the right length.

The really surprising thing is that so few people on this side of the world have yet made material of this sort. If they do, and it's monochrome, why not videotape for it's cheaper overall?

STAFF DEVELOPMENT ACTIVITIES AT THE UNIVERSITY OF SUSSEX

by Brendan Connors, Michael Eraut, Eric Hewton, Arthur Horton, Carolyn Miller, Education Area, University of Sussex

The purpose of this 'workshop' was to give participants the opportunity to investigate, discuss and criticise the range of staff development and related activities that have arisen at the University of Sussex over the last few years. The Sussex team drew on their experience of discussion, development and evaluation within the university — of teaching an M.A. course in curriculum development in higher education and of research relevant to staff development. It was hoped that much of the initiative would stem from the participants. For this reason an introductory period was devoted to the inspection of relevant documents and to random questioning on an informal basis. A number of discussion topics were then offered, and it was intended that the group should split up if necessary. Though topics were added at the request of participants the starting agenda included the following areas for discussion.

1) Support for Probationers Results of a survey of probationer views and experience of a programme emphasising small group problem-focused discussion.

2) The Relationship between Evaluation and Staff Development Evaluation as a social process involving both personal and organisational development. Links between curriculum development and changes in individual teaching styles. Evaluation-initiated innovation or development-initiated innovation?

3) Advanced Training in Educational Development Findings of a recently completed DES-funded research project which examined training needs across the higher education sector, developed and evaluated an M.A. course for experienced higher education teachers, and experimented with short advanced courses of up to a week's duration.

PARTICIPANT'S REPORT

by Professor Somkid Kaewsonthi, Chulalongkorn University

This session was organised as a small group discussion. We started by introducing ourselves briefly to the group, and this was followed by the presenting of the staff development activities at the University of Sussex. Three main topics were introduced into the discussions: (a) how to organise programmes of staff development, (b) the M. A. programmes, and (c) research in staff development.

It was very beneficial to the participants in this session to learn how they organised the programmes and what types of programmes they have at the University of Sussex. It would have been even more beneficial to us and also to the presenters if time had allowed the participants to present also the types of programmes at their institutions for comparison and discussion. It is not possible for me to comment on the programmes of the University of Sussex since the programmes in each institution depend upon many factors and constraints; i. e. the needs of the staff, the philosophy and policy of the institution, the commitment of the institution to staff development, the origins and the culture of each country, etc. This broader view and experience of staff development teams are the most important and valuable factors. We would have needed much more time and more discussion to share our experience in this theme. We did give some time to talk about the M. A. programme at the University of Sussex and the research in the staff development. These two topics are also interesting but the time was so limited. It was more like presentation and questions rather than discussion for sharing experience.

The overall performance of the presenters and the session was very good. I liked the session very much and wish to have much more time for discussion in each theme to share experiences with the other participants in the session as well.

SEXABOARD: AN EXAMINATION BOARD SIMULATION GAME

by S. Armstrong, J. Cable, T.J. Gaskell, The Polytechnic, Huddersfield

If you have an unshakable belief that before an examinations board can be relied upon to make valid decisions its members must be soundly indoctrinated in rules for proceeding to correct answers to perennial issues, then the workshop was likely to be of little value to you. For you are beyond our help, indeed, beyond redemption. If, on the other hand, like us, you believe that many problems faced by examination boards do not have neat, final answers, then we were sure that you would find the game of interest and relevance.

The aim of Sexaboard is to provide teaching staff, who have little or no experience of the examinations board situation, with a working understanding of its processes and purposes. Many of the former are usually dictated by complex, rule-bound structures of convention which overshadow the latter. The underpinning concepts are often vaguely defined and rarely, if ever, referred to during the course of an examination board's deliberations. As such, it is dubious to assume, as is normally the case, that these processes and purposes are best inculcated in the real situation where the novitiate is left to learn through his flounderings.

At the same time, the very essence of the game is seated in a belief that these concepts lend readily to instruction which involves the subjectivity of conflicting views and decision-making. The scenario of the game has been designed to bring participants to realise that, more often than not, an examinations board needs to seek ongoing solutions — solutions which reflect a recognition of aspects such as student background, attitudes, situation, aspirations and level of maturation. This has involved structuring a situation in which each participant comes to recognise the emergence of alternative solutions and conclusions.

Our experience has been like that of the growing number of the users of Sexaboard, that the game meets with a large measure of success in bringing the novitiate to terms with that which is the ritual of the examinations board.

PARTICIPANT'S REPORT

by B. McInnes, University of Sydney

This workshop was attended by about ten people, all of whom appeared to agree that it was an interesting and useful experience. Most of the time was spent participating in the simulated examination board and little time was spent in discussing its value and applicability.

A measure of the intrinsic interest of the game was the thoroughness with which the participants entered into the rôle playing; some even managed successfully to adopt dual personalities (the need for this arose from the shortage of players). Most appeared to be experienced campaigners, and, as such, quite capable of allowing discussion of student performance to bog down in trivialities: the chairman found it necessary more than once to remind the Board that the external examiners had to leave soon to catch the 4.20 to London. Although Sexaboard was developed in the immediate context of English polytechnics, participants from European, South African and Australian universities found no difficulty in fitting into the game and relating it to their own experiences.

The impression I gained was that the usefulness of Sexaboard lay not only in providing experience for the novice but also in setting up a situation in which the veteran examination-board practitioner could review his attitudes (prejudices) free from the stress of the real Board. It seemed that a Sexaboard session would provide a very suitable springboard for discussions on the how, what and why of assessment procedures in a staff-training course.

REPERTORY GRID TECHNIQUES APPLIED TO THE IDENTIFICATION OF ASPECTS OF PEDAGOGIC STYLE CONTRIBUTING TO TEACHER EFFECTIVENESS

by Terence R. Keen, Education Officer, Plymouth Polytechnic

Much research has concentrated on the outcomes of the teaching-learning experience in order to try and measure teacher effectiveness. Whilst it cannot be denied that these researchers have recorded some interesting observations, I showed that this perspective on the problem presents a less than complete picture.

My research methodology was developed primarily to examine in detail the ways in which different teachers play their roles in the teaching-learning process and to explore the perspectives of students on the variety of pedagogic styles utilised. It rapidly became evident that combining repertory grid techniques with micro-teaching analysis not only achieved the primary objective, but also provided a valid means of evaluating teaching effectiveness.

In using the technique the teacher is invited to specify, on cards, the names of certain other teachers (anonymity is assured). He is guided in his selection by certain directives. In total, he will complete thirteen such cards. He then views a prepared videotape of excerpts from lectures and whilst watching, is encouraged to make notes, relating to each of the teachers he observes, on further cards.

The normal elicitation procedures for repertory grids are then used, by presenting triads of cards to the teacher, from which he formulates a bi-polar construct subsequently utilised to rate all of the twenty coded cards. The process is repeated between ten and twenty times to complete the grid. The completed grid is then subjected to a principal component analysis from which groupings of the elements (i.e. cards) can be identified. At this stage, it is relatively easy to isolate the constructs used by the teacher to describe the groupings identified. Experience has shown that this information, when fed back to the teacher, provides an adequate means of self-evaluation and frequently provokes overt changes in the pedagogic style, as a direct result of involvement in the technique.

Staff development is interpreted in many ways, ranging from the provision of formal induction courses for new recruits to the teaching profession, to providing study leave for research or other activities. I firmly believe the improvement of teaching effectiveness is the prime means of facilitating staff development, and this workshop proposes one means by which teaching effectiveness may be evaluated and subsequently improved.

PARTICIPANT'S REPORT

by D. Harris, University of Bath

A development of Kelly's repertory grids technique was described for use with teachers of Physics. The grid was based on 21 constructs, using descriptions some of which were supplemented by short videotape excerpts to clarify characteristics. The grid was used with teachers and their students. Using extensive statistical techniques examples were elaborated from a handout based on computer print-outs. On the basis of the evidence provided it was suggested that a suitable system had been devised for Physics teachers, for which a very much simpler print-out would be used. It was tentatively proposed by the presenter that the scheme had potential for other disciplines.

Discussion Points

The statistical techniques were queried because it was suggested that certain assumptions were made in relation to the methods of applying the techniques. Dr. Keen argued that the techniques were dependent purely on the elements and the constructs. The main discussion centred round the details of the scheme and the cost in terms of designing the system, the use of the computer, and the time spent by users and their students. The evidence of effectiveness from teachers who had used the system was subjective and anecdotal.

The general impression was that the group were most interested, but cautious because of the implications of cost in staff time and student time. No doubt like all other groups looking at staff development they felt that the easier and cheaper solution the better. This method is not cheap nor is it easy, but at least it uses the teachers' own constructs rather than pontifications by experts.

MICROTEACHING AS AN ANALOGUE OF LECTURING

by G. A. Brown, University of Nottingham

This workshop was concerned with the use of microteaching in the training of lecturers in lecturing techniques. The workshop focused sharply upon the central activity of lecturing explaining. There was a brief introduction to the topic and then an opportunity to view and discuss videotaped explanations. Participants were also introduced to ways of observing and analysing explanations. The workshop ended with a brief discussion of the correspondence between microteaching activities and lecturing.

PARTICIPANT'S REPORT

by B. C. Stace, University of Surrey

This session on Microteaching by George Brown was, for me, the most useful and interesting of the conference.

The workshop was opened with a comparison between the original Dwight Allen (Stanford, 1964) microteaching procedure and that of George Brown (Nottingham, 1970). In the former a specific teaching skill is isolated and practiced in a teach-critique-reteach cycle. In the latter the teaching activity consists of a four-minute presentation of an 'explanation', which is conceived as a scaled-down lecture and in which all appropriate skills are used. There is also a critique stage, in which the videotape is observed and discussed, and a reteach stage.

At Nottingham microteaching is part of an initial course for new staff but some microteaching is also offered to experienced teachers. In addition to the three stages already mentioned a talk is given on designing, presenting and analysing 'explanations' and also brief live demonstrations of lecturing styles are provided (George Brown demonstrated two to us).

During the conference workshop the idea of the four-minute explanation as an analogue of a 55-60 minute lecture was presented. It is considered that the four minutes should consist of an explanation because lecturing is 'sustained explaining' and furthermore 'explaining is giving understanding to another'. These ideas and this approach were vigorously discussed as was the choice of four minutes for the duration of the presentation. Participants in the activities at Nottingham are given forms for analysis of personal behaviour and mannerisms of the lecturers and also for the analysis of the content. Examples of transcripts of 'explanations' which had been analysed with the aid of these instruments were presented. We also saw some 'before' and 'after' videotapes of staff in action. The discussion on these considered, among other matters, the question of the persistence of improvement but little is known about this important matter.

10. CLOSING PLENARY SESSION

Evaluation of the Conference

Dr. C. C. Matheson (Co-ordinating and Research Officer, Co-ordinating Committee for the Training of University Teachers, University of East Anglia)

EVALUATION OF CONFERENCE

by Dr. C. C. Matheson, Co-ordinating and Research Officer, Co-ordinating Committee for the Training of University Teachers, The Registry, University of East Anglia, Norwich

Introduction

The conference programme contained, apart from opening and closing plenaries, seven 'formal' sessions (using twenty-seven speakers) and eight workshop sessions. Because sessions were run in parallel, each participant could choose to attend three of these fifteen sessions.

Almost 40 per cent of the 180 participants came from universities within the UK. The remainder came equally from polytechnics, from other areas of higher and further education and from abroad.

Evaluation

It was felt that participants attending a conference on staff development, especially one offering such sessions as 'Staff Development through Evaluation', should be given an opportunity within the framework of the conference to evaluate the conference, not only in order to review their own perceptions of the conference but also to provide feedback which could be used in planning future conferences. Accordingly, during the closing plenary, participants were invited to evaluate the conference, first individually and then in groups of three to four. No criteria for evaluation were stipulated, instead, participants were invited to put forward relevant criteria and to rate these on the scale, +3 +2 +1 0 -1 -2 -3, where zero indicated no opinion. There was also an opportunity for participants to rate the conference over-all and the conference publicity on a similar scale. Space was provided on the evaluation forms for more general comment on the conference.

Summary of Responses

125 individual evaluation sheets and 33 group evaluation sheets were returned for analysis. The 897 criteria put forward by participants for evaluation of the conference and the 86 comments on the conference fell into three broad areas relating to :

a) the conference programme;
b) the conference process;
c) the conference organisation.

These areas could be further divided as shown in Table 1 which indicates the frequency of scale ratings for a particular criterion, together with the frequency of critical and favourable comment.

A table of such brevity cannot show the nuances found within the criteria. However these are indicated in Table 2 (p. 154) where some of the comments made by participants are quoted.

Conclusion

This evaluation raises a number of questions for further discussion. Firstly, in general:

i) Should formal conference evaluation routinely form a part of staff development conferences?

ii) How should such an evaluation be conducted?

iii) What are the relevant criteria for evaluation?

Secondly, in relation to this conference:

iv) Were the conference aims and objectives both appropriate and clearly identified?

v) Was the format of the conference consistent with its aims?

vi) Did the conference programme provide participants with the appropriate means of achieving the objectives?

vii) Did this evaluation assist participants and conference organisers to assess and review the conference?

TABLE 1: Rated Criteria for Evaluation of the Conference

	RATING							COMMENT	
CRITERION	+3	+2	+1	0	-1	-2	-3	Critical	Favourable
Conference programme									
Conference publicity	4	35	38	29	14	6	4	6	-
Conference theme and objectives	-	1	1	1	-	2	1	6	-
Breadth of coverage	9	20	5	-	3	-	-	-	1
Parallel sessions	2	5	1	-	6	8	7	23	-
Structured programme	-	1	1	-	-	1	2	-	-
Conference pace	4	3	3	-	6	9	3	20	1
Conference process									
Conference over-all	6	61	42	2	4	2	2	-	-
Clarity of definition of staff development	-	1	2	-	4	2	3	4	-
Standard of papers	6	15	6	1	1	1	-	-	-
Standard of speakers	5	19	6	1	1	3	-	1	-
Exhibitions	4	13	7	2	2	1	-	1	-
Workshops	1	3	1	-	-	-	-	-	-
Stimulation	4	3	6	1	2	-	-	-	1
Relevance	2	12	7	-	2	-	-	-	1
Usefulness in institutional role	-	6	13	2	-	1	-	-	-
Information	3	17	4	-	-	-	-	-	-
New ideas	3	13	18	1	4	-	2	-	-
New techniques	1	5	6	-	-	-	-	-	-
Opportunity for participation	1	6	6	1	8	8	2	5	-
Opportunity for exchange of ideas	4	8	5	4	2	2	-	-	-
Opportunity to give own ideas	-	-	1	-	2	-	1	-	-
Opportunity for informal contact	22	38	9	1	2	3	1	-	-
Opportunity for small group discussion	-	-	-	-	3	1	2	7	-
Reference to student perspective	-	-	-	-	2	-	-	3	-
Theoretical perspectives on staff development	1	2	6	-	9	5	3	7	-
Emphasis on teaching competence	-	-	-	-	-	1	1	7	-
Variety of participants	6	1	-	-	1	-	-	-	-
Conference organisation									
Organisation	20	18	14	-	-	2	-	-	-
Signposting	-	-	-	-	-	3	6	1	-
Board, lodgings & environment	19	23	14	3	4	2	4	-	-
Heating	-	-	-	-	1	5	1	-	-

TABLE 2: A Selection of Quoted Comments on the Conference

Conference theme and objectives	"Primary task of conference unclear — to report and exchange research or to 'sell' views of what should be done in staff training?". "Need for keynote lecture — e.g. 'what is staff development?' ". "Lack of explicit statement on objectives". "Aims of conference unclear".
Conference publicity	"Final programme not detailed enough". "Abstracts should be available for all sessions". "Publicity should make clear who will speak on what".
Breadth of coverage	"A good, rich variety of themes, topics and workshop activities for people to choose from".
Parallel sessions	"Frustration regarding inability to attend sessions which clashed". "Disappointed in being unable to participate in some of the options". "Felt deprived of too many parallel sessions". "As a 'delegated representative' felt my duty was to attend the more formal sessions". "Separate time for workshops is important".
Structured programme	"Need flexibility of format to allow for emergent needs during conference". "Too formal organisation". "Awareness of participants' needs lacking".
Conference pace	"Too much squeezed into too little time". "Enough material for three conferences". "Conference generally over concentrated — contributions too truncated".

	"Insufficient time to deal with any single contribution in detail".
	"Need another day".
	"Time allocated to sessions too little".
	"Time could have been used more intensively".
Clarity of definition of staff development	"I had expected there to be clearer consideration of staff development needs, objectives and methods and possible evaluation of methods. Conference illustrated the range of different concepts and approaches but with little definition".
	"Notion of staff development (as presented in conference) seemed quite diffuse".
Standard of speakers	"One might have looked for a higher standard of presentation. If so one would have been disappointed".
Stimulation	"Means of personal academic stimulation".
	"Stimulating new ideas".
	"Stimulating me to some action".
	"Stimulus for new enquiry".
Relevance	"Relevance to staff development".
	"Relevance to my own work".
	"Relevance to conference theme".
	"Relevance of sessions to purpose of conference".
Usefulness in institutional role	"Ideas of conference applicable in own institution".
	"Usefulness as a course developer".
	"Own 'staff development' ".
	"Provoked thoughts about my role in my institution".
Information	"Sensing 'state of the art' ".

New ideas	"Raises understanding of problems involved". "Broadens participants' perceptions". "Increases awareness of key issues".
New techniques	"Opportunity to see new techniques in operation". "Experience of practical activities and techniques".
Opportunity for participation	"Insufficient time for discussion after presentations". "Not enough time for useful discussions". "Not enough involvement".
Opportunity for small group discussion	"More group work needed". "It can be better to have more small group discussions".
Reference to student perspective	"General impression of over-concern with teaching — under-concern with learning". "Could usefully be student participation in conference, since student reactions carry implications for the appropriateness of staff activity". "Could have paid more attention to the need for feedback from undergraduates — is student evaluation of lectures too hot a potato? ".
Theoretical perspectives on staff development	"Discussion on critical issues making me question my assumptions". "Lack of research input (which presumably is a function of the Society for Research into Higher Education) ". "Evidence of low level of awareness of literature of staff development, even among the contributors".

Emphasis on teaching competence	"Conference organisers chose to concentrate on staff development in its relationship to to teaching competence. Would have liked to hear and discuss more about staff development of other staff people than teachers and of teachers with administrative responsibility". "Training of teachers stressed expense of management training and organisational context of staff development". "Title of conference could well have been 'Teacher Training' ".

APPENDICES

APPENDIX I: LIST OF EXHIBITS

Dr. S. Armstrong (Huddersfield Polytechnic) — 'Sexaboard'

*D. Butts (Jordanhill College) — 'An experiment in distance teaching'

R. F. Clarke (University of Manchester) — 'Staff development policy and the practice in some developing countries'

Dr. F. W. Parrett (Queens University, Ontario) — 'Ontario's first major workshop for university teachers'

Dr. J. P. Powell (University of New South Wales) — 'The use of 'trigger' films in developing teaching skills'

P. Ramsden (University of Lancaster) — 'The contribution of student feedback to staff development'

Ms. J. Riley (Open University) — 'There are many ways of teaching grandmothers to suck eggs'

Ms. F. C. Wildon (University of East Anglia) — 'The activities of the Working Unit for the training of University Teachers, University of East Anglia'

C. C. de Winter Hebron (Newcastle upon Tyne Polytechnic) — 'The contribution of educational development services in polytechnics'

J. Towner (University of Surrey) — 'Postgraduate diploma in teaching and learning in higher education'

Ms. J. Tait (Brighton Polytechnic) — 'SCEDSIP' and 'Educational developments at Brighton Polytechnic'

*Dr. G. Manwaring (Dundee College of Education) — 'Materials for staff development'

A. Schofield (University of London University Teaching Methods Unit) — 'University of London University Teaching Methods Unit'

D. Hounsell (University of Lancaster) — 'The contribution of research on teaching and learning to educational development'

D. Harris (University of Bath) — 'Water dripping on a stone — the use of printed materials in staff training and development'

*Note: These were demonstrated by M. Lopez of the Institute for Educational Technology, University of Surrey

APPENDIX II : LIST OF PARTICIPANTS

Jane Abercrombie
Dr. David Armstrong (Open University)
Dr. Stuart Armstrong (Huddersfield Polytechnic)
Sandra Ashman (North London Polytechnic)
D. E. Aston (Association of University Teachers)
G. F. Badley (Liverpool Polytechnic, School of Education)
P. A. Baynes (Goldsmiths' College)
Professor Tony Becher (University of Sussex)
Dr. F. D. Bell (UMIST)
Dr. D. J. Bennett (Australian National University)
Dr. David Billing (Council for National Academic Awards)
Professor Paul Black (Chelsea College)
Brian Blake (University of Lancaster)
Dr. Donald Bligh (University of Exeter)
John Blythe (Tameside College of Technology)
N. C. Boreham (University of Manchester)
Philip Bradbury (North East London Polytechnic)
Dr. George Brown (University of Nottingham)
Joe Brown (Hull College of Higher Education)
Chris Burdon (North London Polytechnic)
Dr. Dietrich Brandt (Hochschuldidaktisches Zentrum Aachen)
Ron Britton (Eastbourne College of Education)
Professor J. B. Broadbent (University of East Anglia)
Jonathan Bursey (University of Newcastle upon Tyne)
Jon Cable (Huddersfield Polytechnic)
Brian Cane (City of Liverpool Polytechnic, C. F. Mott Wing)
Mike Capper (Victoria University of Wellington, New Zealand)
Dr. J. F. Chambers (Western Australian Institute of Technology)
Miss T. Chiverton (City of London Polytechnic)
Dr. Jean Clark (Melbourne State College)
R. F. Clarke (University of Manchester)
C. R. Coles (University of Southampton)
Gerald Collier (formerly Principal, Bede College, Durham)
Dr. Robert Collin (University of Western Australia)
Dr. John Cowan (Heriot-Watt University)
Dr. R. Cowell (Sunderland Polytechnic)
Dr. Roy Cox (University Teaching Methods Unit)
Cdr. T. K. Cropper (HMS Nelson (RNSETT))

Dr. Eric Debney (Bolton College of Education (Technical))
C.R. Doberty (North East London Polytechnic)
Professor Paul Dressel (State University of Michigan)
S. C. Driver (University of Melbourne)
Ralph Eaton (Preston Polytechnic)
Professor Brigitte Eckstein (Technische Hochschule Aachen)
D. G. Edwards (Bolton College of Education (Technical))
J. Elfick (Goroka Teachers College)
Dr. B.J. Elliott (University of Stirling)
Professor Lewis Elton (University of Surrey)
Jeremy Evans
Leo Evans (The City University)
Norman Evans (Bishop Lonsdale College)
Dr. T.W. Field (Armidale College of Advanced Education, Australia)
Professor Thomas Finkenstaedt (Bayer. Staatinst. f. Hochschulplanung und Hochschulforschung, München)
Colin Flood Page (University of Bradford)
Dennis Fox (Trent Polytechnic)
Dr. Chris Furedy (University of York, Canada)
Alan George (North London Polytechnic)
G.O. Gibb (University of Edinburgh)
Graham Gibbs (Open University)
Dr. D.R. Gibson (Cambridge Institute of Education)
Åke Göransson (University of Lund)
Peter Grainge (Bishop Otter College)
Count Lysander de Grandy (University of Southampton Students' Union)
Peter Green (Bishop Lonsdale College)
Harriet Greenaway (North London Polytechnic)
Dr. Penny Griffin (Middlesex Polytechnic)
Professor W. F. Gutteridge (University of Aston)
Trevor Habeshaw (Bristol Polytechnic)
Dr. Ernest Hankamer (University of Maryland)
Alan Harding (University of Bradford)
Dr. Duncan Harris (University of Bath)
D. Harte (University of Newcastle upon Tyne)
H. Heisler (Lanchester Polytechnic)
Dr. Hugh Helm (Rhodes University)
Norman Henry (Royal Melbourne Inst. of Technology)
Dr. L.J. Herbst (Teesside Polytechnic)
G.D. Hermann (Brunel University)
Guner Hoglund (Karolinska Institutet, Stockholm)
Betty Hollinshead (Manchester Polytechnic)
Dai Hounsell (University of Lancaster)
Ian Hutchings (Assn. of Polytechnic Teachers)
Hans Jalling (National Board of Universities & Colleges, Stockholm)
David Jaques (UTMU)
Dr. B.V.E. Jones (Middlesex Polytechnic)
Edward Jones (Inter-University Council for H.E. Overseas)

Professor Somid Kaewsonthi (Chulalongkorn University)
Terence Keen (Plymouth Polytechnic)
Michael Kendall (University of London)
Dr. E. Kerr (Council for National Academic Awards)
Jessica Kidd (University of Newcastle upon Tyne)
Mrs. S. Kirkhope (University of Bath)
Dr. Seppo Kontiainen (UTMU University of London)
Dr. Jan Kucirek (University of Surrey)
Dr. H. A. Lewis (University of Leeds)
Lionel Lane (Middlesex Polytechnic)
David Lovatt (Middlesex Polytechnic)
Mrs. J. Lublin (Lincoln Institute, Australia)
Professor A. J. Lyon (University of Hong Kong)
Esmé Lyon (Chinese University of Hong Kong)
Ray McAleese (University of Aberdeen)
Gordon McGregor (Bishop Otter College)
Dr. Brian McInnes (University of Sydney)
P. J. McVey (University of Surrey)
E. W. Malone (St. Mary's College of Education)
Mrs. D. Martin (Assn. of University Teachers)
Dr. C. C. Matheson (University of East Anglia)
Dr. Gordon Miller (University of London)
Stewart Miller (University of Kent)
Dr. Marcel Mirande (University of Amsterdam)
A. M. Moon (Ulster College)
Dr. Kin-chok Mun (Chinese University of Hong Kong)
Dr. R. C. Mylward (Bolton College of Education (Technical))
Andrew Northedge (Open University)
Miss K. L. Oglesby (University of Sheffield)
Dr. P. A. Ongley (University of Aston)
K. Onion (Trent Polytechnic)
Jose Orellana (Central University, Caracas — Venezuela)
Dr. David O'Sullivan (University of Sussex)
Marjorie Painter (Oxford Polytechnic)
Dr. Fred Parrett (Queen's University, Ontario)
D. A. B. Pearson (Laurentian University, Ontario)
Dr. J. M. Perz (University of Toronto)
Ronald Pickering (Wolverhampton Polytechnic)
J. M. Popkin (Oxford Polytechnic)
Dr. J. P. Powell (University of New South Wales)
Paul Ramsden (University of Lancaster)
Professor Dent Rhodes (Illinois State University)
Denis Rice (University of Leicester)
Wolf Reiss (Johann Wolfgang Goethe-Universitat)
Judith Riley (Open University)
Angela Ringguth (North London Polytechnic)
Professor U. Ritter (Johann Wolfgang Goethe-Universitat)

T. J. Roberts (North London Polytechnic)
Sarah Robinson (UTMU, University of London)
Glynnis Rodgers (Sheffield City Polytechnic)
David Ross (University of Bradford)
Jean Rossiter (North East London Polytechnic)
Dr. Desmond Rutherford (University of Birmingham)
Anne-Marie Rydell (University of Stockholm)
Susan Sayer (Salford University)
R. Schofield (Brunel University)
P. G. Scopes (Avery Hill College)
Gordon Scott (Bolton College of Education (Technical))
Peter Seaborne (Bulmershe College of Higher Education)
Felicity Seelhoff (University of East Anglia)
Lu Sinclair (University of Singapore)
Dr. Arie Smit (Educational Media Institute, Utrecht)
B. M. Smith (University of Sussex)
Don Snow
Dr. Brian Stace (University of Surrey)
Dr. Richard Startup (University College, Swansea)
J. Stoddart (Hull College of Higher Education)
Joanna Tait (Brighton Polytechnic)
Gordon Taylor (Bishop Lonsdale College)
A. G. Thomas (Ealing Technical College)
B. Thorne (University of East Anglia)
A. Todd (Newcastle upon Tyne Polytechnic)
Jerry Towner (University of Surrey)
Dr. Stuart Trickey (Sheffield City Polytechnic)
Dr. P. J. C. Veltman (Rijksuniversiteit Utrecht)
Elena Villarroel (University of Central Venezuela)
David Walker (Times Higher Education Supplement)
Hugh Walmsley (North London Polytechnic)
Dr. Janek Wankowski (University of Birmingham)
Dr. J. W. L. Warren (Leicester Polytechnic)
David Warren Piper (University of London)
Wolff-Dietrick Webler (Universitat Bielefeld)
M. F. Westcott-Lewis (Riverina College of Advanced Education)
Jean Whittaker (Bishop Grosseteste College)
Dr. D. Wildon (University of East Anglia)
Mrs. D. Williams (Portsmouth Polytechnic)
G. L. Williams (Sheffield Polytechnic)
N. R. Winterburn (The City University)
C. C. de Winter Hebron (Newcastle Polytechnic)
Vincent Worth (Open University)
Mantz Yorke (Manchester Polytechnic)